DEPENDENCE IN MAN

DEPENDENCE IN MAN
A Psychoanalytic Study

Henri Parens and Leon J. Saul

Routledge
Taylor & Francis Group

LONDON AND NEW YORK

First published in 1971 by International Universities Press
Published 2014 by Karnac Books Ltd.

Published 2018 by Routledge
2 Park Square, Milton Park, Abingdon, Oxon OX14 4RN
711 Third Avenue, New York, NY 10017, USA

Routledge is an imprint of the Taylor & Francis Group, an informa business

British Library Cataloguing in Publication Data
A C.I.P. for this book is available from the British Library

ISBN: 978-1-78220-159-5

To our wives and children

CONTENTS

PART III
CLINICAL CONSIDERATIONS

Acknowledgements

We are indebted to Dr. Calvin F. Settlage, who took time from a crowded schedule to subject our manuscript to careful criticisms when it was in its initial stage, and who brought it to the attention of Dr. Margaret S. Mahler. We find it difficult to properly express our gratitude to Dr. Mahler. In the midst of writing the first volume of her important work, *On Human Symbiosis and the Vicissitudes of Individuation*, she was generous enough, not only to evaluate our manuscript and offer helpful suggestions which we adopted, but also to write the Foreword. Dr. W. Godfrey Cobliner recommended changes, and these, too, we have gratefully incorporated.

Our thanks go to Dr. Harry F. Harlow for his friendly comments on our discussion (Chapter 2) of his work.

We thank Mrs. Irene Azarian for her kind encouragement and constructive suggestions. To our editor, Mrs. Natalie Altman, goes our deep appreciation for her careful preparation of the manuscript. It was a pleasure to work with her.

1

We are pleased to acknowledge our debt to Miss Sandra Malazar and her staff at the Philadelphia Child Guidance Clinic for typing and retyping the manuscript.

To Rachel A. Parens, who listened to our thoughts before they were put to paper and who, by editing the first draft of our manuscript, helped determine the character of the existing work, our deepest gratitude.

Foreword

It is a pleasure to write a foreword to what is a very timely book, one which promises to have significance for a large audience.

Drs. Parens and Saul are addressing themselves to the universal phenomenon of dependence in man, a subject central to my own studies on human development. They have, with incomparable thoroughness, combed the psychoanalytic literature to present the reader with all the ramifications and variations of dependence, including its obverse. Their review strongly supports Freud's theories on the origins of human dependence, and they have carefully culled the work of Freud and his followers, presenting it from their own perspective, so that psychological functioning can be apprehended with greater depth in a wider panorama. In addition, they offer a condensed review of recent contributions in ethology, including work on primates.

Dependence is not only a prime determinant of behavior; it is also a powerful inducer of development. By introducing new concepts, Drs. Parens and Saul have added significance to that thesis. They have set themselves the task of tracing dependence and its vicissitudes through the life cycle, from the early mother-infant dyad, the triad of the oedipal period, through adolescence, maturity, and senescence. In the process, the dimensions, co-ordinates, and variables of dependence emerge in all their richness. The authors give due emphasis to dynamic and structural considerations. Their clinical examples provide cogent illustrations of how defense mechanisms are mobilized in response to what the individual conceives of as a threat to his autonomy and separateness. In these few lines one can hardly do justice to the scope and importance of this encyclopedic book. Whether the reader's interest is theoretical or clinical, he will be richly rewarded and stimulated.

Drs. Parens and Saul have written a much needed treatise. In our rapidly changing world, where the interdependence of man is constantly increasing, where our separateness and identity seem about to become engulfed by the complexities of new social and technological developments, this book allows us to recognize a distinct outline of the phenomenon of dependence as a reality in psychological functioning. In addition, the concept of dependence will help us to order many clinical manifestations in different contexts. I can recommend this work wholeheartedly to all those who are seriously concerned with this increasingly important subject.

Margaret S. Mahler, M.D.

Introduction

As psychoanalytic work continues to expand, we are pushed to further avenues of exploration. The extensive literature on the metapsychology of object relations, of identification and psychic structure formation, of problems of anxiety, suggests that we view these concepts from the aspect of psychic dependence.

The clinician constantly encounters problems arising from insufficiently-resolved conflicts which have at their core a nucleus of unyielding dependence. Analysts often deal with excessive dependence in the transference, but they have not established for it a place in the literature commensurate with its importance. Mahler's formulations on symbiosis and separation-individuation are a large step toward remedying that lack.

Excessive dependence is of central significance in the "oral-dependent" character and the chemically-addicted. In addition, even clinically, the area of the influence of dependence is greater than is generally recognized. For example, some of our most severe disorders stem, to an important degree, from *defects in normal dependence* on the object: "primary" and "secondary" autism arise from a disastrously insufficient cathexis of objects; so do the schizoid and possibly some borderline states (Rosenfeld and Sprince, 1963). Many an antisocial character has at its core the disavowal of early object cathexes and a rejection of early infantile needs for love and protection from the parental environment. Take also the miscarriage of infantile dependence on the object that we see in symbiotic childhood psychosis (Mahler, 1952; Mahler & Gosliner, 1955) where that dependence does not yield to the normal process of separation-individuation (Mahler, 1968b).

However, our concern here is not only the large and complex role dependence plays in the etiology of neurosis (Freud, 1940) and in disordered character formation. More important, *we want to draw attention to the fact of normative dependence*, to its influence on the development of the psychic organization, and to its lifelong presence in man.

Perhaps because dependence is associated with the state of helplessness characteristic of infancy and childhood, its appearance in adults is often regarded as pathological. The social attitude towards dependence, in our culture, tends to be negative. Children are often prematurely pushed toward independence, and conflicts arising from excessive frustration of dependent needs may be disregarded. Indeed, many see even dependence in the infant as a problem. Nearly three decades ago, Ribble observed: "The bugbear of emotional dependency is, like thumb-sucking, a great problem in the mind of many a thoughtful parent" (1943, p. 110). Perhaps we tend to by-pass or simply deny its ubiquity because, as Freud observed (1913, 1926, 1927, 1930, 1940), it reveals our most vulnerable attributes: that we are too often helpless against forces greater than ourselves and that we so often deeply need others for

optimal psychic functioning and for a reasonable existence. It seems that the term, when used, is generally employed pejoratively. An exploration of the metapsychology of dependence might serve to modify our view of it.

That the child's helplessness and dependence is of great
consequence to the nature of his adaptation and psychic
development has often before been stated. Freud formulated its relevance to psychic structure formation in 1923,
delineated some of its relations to anxiety in 1926, to the
origins of religious belief in 1927 and 1930, and advised in
1939 (1940) that we formulate and account for its role in
the development of neurosis. Mahler (1963), who holds
"that a lifelong, albeit, diminishing, emotional dependence
on the mother is a universal truth of human existence" (p.
307, our italics), has drawn attention to the importance of
the fact that the "libidinal availability of the mother, because of the emotional dependence of the child, facilitates
the optimal unfolding of innate potentialities" in him (p.
322). She has noted (1963), as has Jacobson (1954,
1964), the far-reaching influence of the character of the
earliest dependence on the object to the ultimate development of the individual's psychic organization: "I believe it
is *from the symbiotic phase* of the mother-infant dual
unity that those experiential precursors of individual beginnings are derived which, together with inborn constitutional factors, determine every human individual's unique
somatic and psychological make-up" (p. 307; italics
added). Spitz (1950) referring to the third quarter of the
first year, when the libidinal object appears, says, "It is at
this turning point of the development that the basic security and the basic insecurity of the child and later on of
the adult is laid down. Here is the beginning of so many
severe neurotic and psychotic conditions, and it is therefore here that we have to take our stand: *principiis obsta*"

(p. 141). Erikson (1950, 1959) pointed to "basic trust", and Benedek (1949, 1956) to "confident expectation" at this phase of development, noting the fundamental importance of this earliest "ego state" to the eventual total personality.

Fairbairn (1954) and Winnicott (1965) have each stated that a psychoanalytic developmental psychology must take into account the fact of the child's dependence. Fairbairn emphasized the centrality of dependence in the development of psychic functioning, of object relations, and in libido theory (1941, 1951, both in Fairbairn, 1954, e.g., see pp. 34-35). Winnicott (1965), in an introduction to a collection of his papers, writes: "Ego-psychology only makes sense if based firmly on the fact of dependence" (p. 9). He formulates dependence as being at birth "absolute," then between 6 months to 2 years of age, follows a phase of "relative" dependence, which is in turn followed by a broadly extended phase "toward independence." And he concludes, "Adults must be expected to be continuing the process of growing and of growing up since they do but seldom reach to full maturity" (p. 92). Fairbairn (1954) too suggested such a timetable and relative states of dependence.

Zetzel (1955) discussed briefly the theories of Fairbairn, M. Balint and M. Klein, pointing out that the theoretical work of these authors derives from

> the primary and basic importance of the child's early relationship with the mother. All [these] authors . . . have taken this admittedly fundamental observation as the basis for theoretical hypotheses as to the nature and the development of object relations as a whole. To a greater or lesser extent, each of them puts forth the point of view that a theory of object relations based on the recognition that the infant is from the start of life dependent on an external object, necessitates considerable modification of analytic

theory. It is a matter of considerable doubt as to how far this basic premise ... necessarily carries with it an inevitable alteration of basic theory [p. 536].

These comments recommend that we focus upon the character of the child's earliest adaptation to helplessness and, more specifically, to the influences (some of them most salutary) of the child's dependence on the development of his psychic organization, as well as to a consideration of dependence not only as a force operative in childhood, but also in the life of the normal adult.

When we speak of dependence we mean the need each human has, whether child, adolescent, or adult, for a libidinal object relation in order to insure his optimal psychic functioning. This study is an attempt to bridge the gap between our recognition of the existence of dependence and our understanding of it. It has left us with perhaps more questions than answers. We hope to stimulate interest in some of the problems we have raised here, and we will feel our purpose served if the propositions we advance open broader areas for investigation by others.

PART I

A STUDY OF
FREUD'S WRITINGS

1. A Study of Freud's Writings on Dependence in Man

Although dependence is implied in much of what Freud wrote, nowhere do we find the subject treated explicitly. The word dependence appears neither in his titles nor in his indices. We have attempted to trace Freud's thoughts on dependence both because they are extensive and because the context in which they appear is germane to, indeed forms the nucleus of, the concepts we propose to investigate further here. It is also known that Freud did not formally elaborate his views on genetic theory. Because the genetic point of view is fundamental to the role dependence plays in psychic development, we want to trace elements of that point of view in his writings before entering upon the body of his thoughts on dependence. We point to two factors inherent in the genetic point of view: that the earliest differentiations of the psychic organization determine later ones; and that later differentiations

13

contain within them the former ones from which they arose, i.e., present and past differentiations coexist.

The genetic principle appears in the concepts of the character of the unconscious. From the cautious statement, "we suspect that [the] narcissistic organization is never wholly abandoned" (1913a, p. 89), Freud proceeds to "immutability and indestructibility are qualities . . . [of the] unconscious" (1913a, p. 94). During this period, Freud (1913b), focusing on the extraordinary importance of the impressions of childhood, had this to say about the unconscious: "none of the infantile mental formations perish. . . . [They] are still demonstrably present in maturity. . . . They are . . . merely overlaid" (p. 184).

In the paper "On Narcissism" and in "Mourning and Melancholia" Freud refers in terms of libido theory to these genetic factors: "As always where the libido is concerned, man has here again shown himself incapable of giving up a satisfaction he had once enjoyed" (1914, p. 94); and, ". . . people never willingly abandon a libidinal position" (1917a, p. 244). Again it seems to come into play in *Beyond the Pleasure Principle* (1920): ". . . the compulsion to repeat must be ascribed to the unconscious repressed" (p. 20). Then comes the significant: *"It seems that an instinct is an urge inherent in organic life to restore an earlier state of things"* (p. 36). This return to "an earlier state" so impressed Freud that he perceived it as a biological, indeed, an organic force. We view this observation as most relevant to the genetic principle.

In 1926 he takes a large step in the direction of stating the concept of the coexistence of former and present constructs in association with the formulation of the danger situation series.

In describing the evolution of the various danger-situations from their prototype, the act of birth, I have no intention of asserting that every later determinant of anxiety completely invalidates the preceding one.... *All these danger-situations and determinants of anxiety can persist side by side* and cause the ego to react to them with anxiety at a period later than the appropriate one [pp. 141-142; italics added].

Four years later, in *Civilization and Its Discontents* speaking of what Mahler (1952), Jacobson (1954), and Benedek (1956) were to later identify as the mother-child symbiosis, Freud (1930) asks: "But have we a right to assume the survival of something that was originally there, alongside with what was later derived from it? [and answers] Undoubtedly.... In the realm of the mind ... what is primitive is ... commonly preserved alongside of the transformed version which has arisen from it" (p. 68). But then he steps back in caution: "Perhaps we ought to content ourselves with asserting that what is past in mental life *may* be preserved and is not *necessarily* destroyed" (p. 71). Freud here refers to the original helplessness and dependence of the child which remain in the adult.

Three years later he observes: "Again and again I have had the impression that we have made too little theoretical use of this fact, established beyond any doubt, of the unalterability by time of the repressed" (1933, p. 74). And in 1937(b) speaking of the advantage the analyst has over the archeologist, he states: "It may ... be doubted whether any psychical structure can really be the victim of total destruction" (p. 260). From the same period (1937a) we find this statement:

Our first account of the development of the libido was that an original oral phase gave way to a sadistic-anal phase and ... in turn [to] a phallic-genital one. Later research has not contradicted this view but corrected it by adding that these replacements do not take place all of a sudden but gradually, so that portions of the earlier organization always persist alongside the more recent one, and even in normal development, the transformation is never complete and residues of earlier libidinal fixations may still be retained in the final configuration [p. 229].

Thus, in 1926 Freud applied the genetic principle to the danger situation series; in 1937 he was applying it to the phases of normal libido development. If we consider, as genetic theory dictates, the relevance of dependence to the development of the psychic organization, we find two points emerging: Dependence, being among the first experiences of the ego, is in a position of developmental primacy. This alone guarantees its conservation among patterns of adaptation and dynamic functioning. Secondly, the protracted duration of childhood further insures the perpetuation of dependence in psychic life from all metapsychological points of view.

DEPENDENCE IN RELATION TO HELPLESSNESS AND ANXIETY

In *An Outline of Psychoanalysis* (1940), Freud observes that:

... in the space of a few years the little primitive creature must turn into a civilized human being. ... This ... can almost never be achieved without the additional help of upbringing, of parental influence, which, as a precursor of the superego, restricts the ego's activity by prohibitions and punishments, and encourages or compels the setting-up of repressions. We must therefore not forget to include the influence of civilization among the determinants of neurosis. ... Since the demands of civilization are represented by family upbringing, we must bear in mind the part played by this biological characteristic of the human species—*the prolonged period of its childhood dependence*—in the etiology of the neuroses [p. 185: italics added].

Although Freud had made frequent references to the importance of man's prolonged childhood dependence nowhere does he give us so clear an assignment to bear in mind the part played by dependence in the etiology of the neuroses. We would add: and in normal psychic development.

Freud's interest in the question of dependence in relation to man's helplessness is evident in three major works which appeared in close succession: *Inhibitions, Symptoms and Anxiety* (1926), *The Future of an Illusion* (1927), and *Civilization and Its Discontents* (1930). The concern with helplessness takes us through the signal theory of anxiety, the series of danger situations and their relation to neurosis; it also takes us to the question of the origins and dynamics of religious ideas. And it touches upon object-relations theory.

1. Dependence and the Danger Situation Series

With the reformulation of the theory of anxiety in 1926, Freud observes the centrality of the ego's helplessness and proposes its chronology. In connection with the danger situation series he notes the importance of the child's initial biologic helplessness and dependence and thence his psychologic dependence on the object. We have not seen this idea so strongly emphasized in his previous writings. The experience of the first danger situation (birth) does not reach consciousness, he states. The next danger situation, fear of the loss of the object, does reach consciousness and is followed by the fear of loss of love from the object.

Development of Theory: The Early Determinants of Danger. In *Inhibitions, Symptoms and Anxiety*, Freud

(1926) proposes that the essence of a traumatic situation is the experience of helplessness of the ego when faced with accumulating excitation with which it cannot cope. Signal anxiety, on the other hand is experienced when the ego feels threatened by being presented with some element of the original traumatic situation. As the editors note, the concept of helplessness of the ego has a long previous history:

> ... in the Project of 1895, Freud enumerates the major needs which give rise to endogenous stimuli calling for discharge—'hunger, respiration and sexuality', and in a later passage remarks that in some conditions this discharge 'requires an alteration in the external world (e.g. the supply of nourishment or the proximity of the sexual object)' which 'at early stages the human organism is incapable of achieving' .... And here Freud comments on the 'original helplessness of human beings' [pp. 81, 82].

Another early statement concerning this issue appears in the *Three Essays* where Freud notes that infantile anxiety arises out of the fear of loss of the love object (1905, p. 224). Eight years later (1913b) he says, regarding infantile anxiety (in accordance with his first theory of anxiety): "[T]he principal function of the mental mechanism is to relieve the individual from tensions created in him by his needs" (p. 186).

In 1921 Freud observes: "Fear in an individual is provoked either by the greatness of a danger or by the cessation of emotional ties. . .; the latter is the case of neurotic fear of anxiety" (p. 97). He then quotes Trotter: "The individual feels incomplete if he is alone" (p. 118). This, Freud notes, is observable also in groups where "loss of the leader . . . brings on the outbreak of panic" (p. 97).

Fear of Loss of the Object. In speaking of the "earliest phobias of infancy," Freud (1926) restates that

These ... can be reduced to a single condition—namely, that of missing someone who is loved and longed for [p. 136]. The reason why the infant in arms wants to perceive the presence of its mother is only because it already knows by experience that she satisfies all its needs without delay. The situation, then, which it regards as a 'danger' ... is that ... of a *growing tension due to need*, against which it is helpless [p. 137].

When the infant has found out by experience that an external, perceptible object can put an end to the dangerous situations ... the content of the danger it fears is displaced from the economic situation on to the condition which determined that situation, viz. the loss of object. It is the absence of the mother that is now the danger; and as soon as that danger arises the infant gives the signal of anxiety, before the dreaded economic situation has set in. This change constitutes a first great step forward in the provision made by the infant for its self-preservation ... [p. 138].

... Anxiety is seen to be a product of the infant's mental helplessness which is a natural counterpart of its biological helplessness. ... There is much more continuity between intra-uterine life and earliest infancy than the impressive caesura of the act of birth would have us believe. What happens is that the child's biological situation as a foetus is replaced for it by a psychical object-relation to its mother [p. 138].

With this Freud spells out the danger situation series. On pages 143 and 146 of *Inhibitions, Symptoms and Anxiety*, Freud does not distinguish between loss of the object and loss of the object's love. However, In Addendum C, (see also p. 155) he suggests that

... the first determinant of anxiety, which the ego itself introduces, is loss of perception of the object (which is equated with loss of the object itself). There is as yet no question of loss of love. Later on, experience teaches the child that the object can be present but angry with it; and then loss of love from the object becomes a new and much more enduring danger and determinant of anxiety [1926, p. 170].

In *Civilization and Its Discontents*, Freud (1930) states that we are threatened with suffering from the external

world and from our relations to others. We suffer if the
external world "refuses to sate our needs" (p. 79). The
object's love assures that the needs will be sated. In *The
Future of an Illusion*, Freud remarks on the importance of
the object (1927, p. 22) along the same line as he did in
Totem and Taboo—a child may expect of his father:
"protection, care and indulgence" (1913a, p. 144). In *Civilization and Its Discontents* (1930) he also observes, the
crushingly superior force of nature, one of the three
sources of suffering for man (p. 77), finds a corollary in
fear of aggression by external authority which is "what
fear of loss of love amounts to, for love is a protection
against this punitive aggression" (p. 128). And later
(1933), "The child is brought up to a knowledge of his
social duties by a system of loving rewards and punishments; he is taught that his security in life depends on his
parents (and afterwards other people) loving him" (p.
164).

In a further elaboration of object love and the early
danger situations, Freud (1933) speaks of the sense of inferiority that comes from feeling unloved. Freud is speaking
here of both the love from the object and the ego's relation to the superego, and he therewith draws attention to
"the importance of a mother's love for the mental life of a
child" (p. 66).

Freud (1933) takes up the fate of these early danger
situations: "In the course of development, the old determinants of anxiety should be dropped, since the situations of
danger corresponding to them have lost their importance
owing to the strengthening of the ego. But this only occurs
most incompletely. Many people are unable to surmount
the fear of loss of love" (p. 88).

This thread appears again in connection with the girl's
reproaches to her mother for not giving her a penis. But

pointing to an earlier ontogenetic period he observes (1933), "The reproach against the mother which goes back furthest is that she gave the child too little milk—which is construed against her as lack of love" (p. 122). "It seems ... that the child's avidity for its earliest nourishment is altogether insatiable, that it never gets over the pain of losing its mother's breast. . ." (p. 122; see also 1940, p. 189). Today we may suggest that the loss relates to the more generalized symbiotic tie to the mother (Mahler, 1968b) and not just to its oral libidinal component. We see here what, we believe, will lead Erikson (1959) to "the lost paradise" and what Mahler has described in her work on symbiosis and the process of separation-individuation (1968b).

In 1940 Freud restates some of his views on the genesis of object relations. The "first object is . . . the child's mother. . . . By her care of the child's body, she becomes its first seducer. In these two relations [(1) gratification of dependent needs and (2) sensuality] lies the root of a mother's importance . . . established unalterably for a whole lifetime as the first and strongest love-object and as the prototype of all later love-relations—for both sexes" (p. 188).

A dozen pages on, he discusses the ultimate role dependence plays in neurosis: "Children are protected against the dangers that threaten them from the external world by ... their parents; they pay for this security by a fear of *loss of love* which would deliver them over helpless to the dangers of the external world" (p. 200). And, as he stated in 1926 in regard to the causation of neurosis: "The biological factor [the long period of helplessness and dependence] ... establishes the earliest situations of danger and creates the need to be loved which will accompany the child through the rest of its life" (p. 155). We believe, this

determinant of anxiety to be the product of the libidinization of the experiences of earliest childhood, where the
biological situation of the fetus is replaced by a psychical
object relation (p. 138).

Comment

In Freud's writings, then, we find the thesis that the
life-preservative function of dependence on the object is
universal in man. Its contributions to psychologic development emerge from the cathexis of the object who gratifies
the needs. Indeed, the recurrence of need forges the cathexis of the object and dependence upon it and secures the
formation of persisting object relations (1921). The clinically recognized psychologic reaction of the budding ego,
separation anxiety, "constitutes a first great step . . . for its
self-preservation" (1921, p. 138). Thus, helplessness leading to anxiety and, in turn, to dependence on the object—
and then on the object's love—is a principal adaptive sequence of earliest childhood. The child early learns to seek
shelter from mounting anxiety by turning to the object.
With this seeking, passive dependence becomes active dependence. With the introduction of anxiety between helplessness and dependence on the object, the dependence
becomes libidinized. We may say that the dependence becomes libidinized if we accept the hypothesis that an object cathexis occurs in an action context and with affective
coloring, in other words, in an experience gestalt (Sandler
et. al., 1962, 1963; Parens, 1970a). The experience gestalt
in the object relation we are discussing here is that of
dependence on the object for gratification of need. It is
clear that the developmental period during which this
adaptive sequence emerges is that during which the danger

situations specific for that period (in the epigenetic sense) arise from dependence: fear of loss of the object and fear of loss of the object's love.

2. Dependence in Relation to Helplessness and to Religious Beliefs

Freud traces important psychological needs for religion to two sources: the first one, presented in *Totem and Taboo* (1913a), arises out of the phylogenetic history of man's father complex and his attempts to deal with it. The second, presented in *The Future of an Illusion* (1927), has its origin in man's biologic, and thence ever-present helplessness. Inasmuch as our focus is on helplessness and dependence, we shall here concern ourselves principally with this second source.

In the first two years of life especially, and long after, the child in his helplessness turns to the auxiliary ego, the object, for protection against excessive anxiety. When man, as an adult, experiences helplessness, he may substitute the psychic constructs he ascribes to religion for the actual parental object.

In *Totem and Taboo*, Freud (1913a) observes that man's acceptance of his smallness and resignation to death are never total. ". . . Some of the primitive belief in omnipotence still survives" (p. 88). In comparing the evolving of *Weltanschauungen* in civilization with the phases of human development, he suggests that "the religious phase would correspond to the stage of object-choice of which the characteristic is a child's attachment to his parents" (p. 90). He states later in the same work that longing for the father constitutes the root of every form of religion (p. 148). Freud commented at this early time upon man's dependence on others for survival, in relation to the father-complex and the latter's role in the formation of religious beliefs. He suggested that in consequence of the father-complex, totemic rite became a covenant between the father and the son wherein the father promised to protect, care for, and indulge his son in return for the son's respect of his—father's—life (pp. 134, 144).

In *The Future of an Illusion* (1927) we find Freud's major observations on the relations of helplessness to man's religious beliefs. He observes that man's helplessness

> has an infantile prototype of which it is only a continuation . . ., helplessness . . . as a small child. . . . Man's helplessness remains and along with it his longing for his father, and the gods[1] [17-18].
>
> Religious ideas have arisen from the same need as have all the other achievements of civilization: from the necessity of defending oneself against the crushingly superior forces of nature [p. 21].

We come then to a most interesting part of the dialogue between the protagonist and Freud. The protagonist says:

> You argue that the humanization[2] of nature is derived from the need to put an end to man's perplexity and helplessness . . . [But recalling the presentation in *Totem and Taboo* (1913a) that religious belief emerges from the communal attempts to solve the father-complex, the protagonist adds:] 'and now you transpose everything that was once the father-complex into terms of help-

---

[1] In accordance with more recent formulations of psychoanalytic theory of child development, often where Freud refers to parenting functions of the father, as of the dependence on the "father," it might be more correct to refer to "parents." Freud, (1923) himself made such a revision in *The Ego and the Id*, p. 31, footnote 1, where he stated in this type of circumstance: "perhaps it would be safer to say . . . 'the parents'."

[2] Humanization: that is, anthropomorphizing by externalizing onto the forces of nature the archaic mental representations of the parents.

lessness; ... explain this transformation. [Freud answers:] In *Totem and Taboo* it was not my purpose to explain the origin of religions, but only of Totemism. ... [He adds that a number of problems concerning the formation of religious beliefs were not touched on in 1913.] I am now trying to add the other, less deeply-concealed part. ... It is, of course, my duty to point out the connecting links between what I said earlier and what I put forward now, between the deeper and the manifest motives, between the father-complex and man's helplessness and need for protection. These connections ... consist in the relation of the child's helplessness to the helplessness of the adult which continues it. ... When the growing individual finds that he is destined to remain a child forever, that he can never do without protection ... he creates for himself ... gods. The defense against childish helplessness is what lends its characteristic features to the adult's reaction to the helplessness which *he* has to acknowledge—a reaction which is precisely the formation of religion [p. 22-24]. [And again in Chapter VI he states,] religious ideas ... [attempt to fulfill] the *oldest, strongest and most urgent* wishes of mankind. The secret of their strength lies in the strength of those wishes. As we already know, the terrifying impression of helplessness in childhood aroused the need for protection—for protection through love—which was provided by the father; and the recognition that this helplessness lasts throughout life made it necessary to cling to the existence of a father, but this time a more powerful one [p. 30; italics added].

In *Civilization and Its Discontents*, Freud (1930) reaffirms these views. The vehicle for this is a reply to his good friend Romain Rolland, who

was sorry I had not properly appreciated the true source of religious sentiments. This, he says, consists in .... a feeling of something limitless, unbounded,—as it were ... 'oceanic' ..., That is to say, it is a feeling of an indissoluble bond, of being one with the external world [p. 64, 65]. [Freud observes:] A feeling can only be a source of energy if it is itself the expression of a strong need. The derivation of religious needs from the infant's helplessness and the longing for the father aroused by it seems to me incontrovertible, especially since the feeling is not simple prolonged from childhood days, but is *permanently sustained* by fear of the superior power of Fate. *I cannot think of any need in childhood as strong as the need for a father's protection.* Thus the part played by the oceanic feeling, which might seek something like the restoration of limitless Narcissism is ousted from a place in the foreground. The origin of the religious attitude can be traced back in clear outlines as far as the feeling of infantile helplessness. There may be something further behind that, but for the present it is wrapped in obscurity [p. 72; italics added].

To look at these thoughts in the light of recent formulations in psychoanalysis is most illuminating. Rolland's description of feelings and the phase of development to which Freud assigns the origin of religious ideas are compatible within the framework of the normal symbiosis formulated by Mahler (1952, 1963, 1965, 1968b). In considering the mystical implication in Rolland's argument, we point to Winnicott's (1953) conceptualization that mystery and mysticism tend to be characteristic of transitional phenomena. The normal symbiosis would meet exactly the required conditions for a period characterized by such transitional phenomena, such mysticism and mystery. It is the developmental period when cognitive and affective structures (Piaget, 1962; Spitz, 1960) differentiate to such a degree, when the ego differentiates sufficiently, that awareness of affects and objects occurs, but affects are experienced grossly and objects are vaguely perceived. It is a period in which beginning secondary process functioning is substantially diluted by primary process functioning. This determines the mysticism and omnipotence of the symbiotic mother-child relationship. It is the phase of development when infantile narcissism engulfs the object within the "symbiotic self-representation" (Parens, 1970a), within the symbiotic membrane (Mahler, 1952), when the boundaries between self and object are vague and the child experiences the tie to his mother powerfully. "A feeling of something limitless," an "indissoluble bond," "being one with the external world" (we could say "symbiotic partner" rather than "external world") most aptly describe Mahler's conceptualizations of the symbiotic child-mother relation as experienced from the child's part. The child's first awareness of helplessness and dependence is at this time manifest in the appearance of separation anxiety. The need and longing for the object has its origin in this period. The intensity of the longing to maintain the symbiotic bond is well-characterized by Erikson's observation that "basic trust" develops and safeguards "against the . . . impressions of having been deprived. . . . divided . . . abandoned . . ." (1959, pp. 60-61) when the gradual dissolution of that bond begins to take place with the process of separation-individuation (Mahler, 1968).

We return to Freud's subsequent observations on the influence and nature of religion.

He states (1933), "we must bear in mind what it undertakes to do for human beings . . . it . . . offers them comfort in unhappiness. [In contrast] , . . . there are many situations in which [science] must leave a man to his suffering and can only advise him to submit to it" (pp. 161, 162). Science, Freud suggests, cannot be the omniscient parent man turns to for "protection, care and indulgence." And he later suggests that the god-creator

> really is the father, with all the magnificence in which he once appeared to the small child. . . . The father . . . protected and watched over [the child] in his feeble and helpless state. . . . When a human being has himself grown up, he knows . . . that he is in possession of greater strength, but his insight into the perils of life has also grown greater, and he rightly concludes that fundamentally he still remains just as helpless and unprotected as he was in his childhood. . . . He . . . harks back to the mnemic image

of the father whom in his childhood he so greatly overvalued. He
exalts the image into a deity and makes it into something contem-
porary and real. The effective strength of this mnemic image and
the persistence of his need for protection jointly sustain his belief
in God [p. 163].

Bearing in mind these last two sentences we cite the
important point Freud makes in *An Outline of Psychoanalysis* with reference to the cathexis of "ideas of objects
with libido." Speaking of the mobility of libido, Freud
(1940) states that, "fixation of the libido to particular
objects . . . often persists throughout life" (p. 15).

We have little doubt that such fixation of libido to mental representations of the archaic parents prevails as an
invariable phenomenon in man, and we suggest, furthermore, that the most tenacious fixation would be associated
with the earliest affective-cognitive experiences starting
with the normal symbiotic phase of development. Freud
(1923) made this point clearly in Chapters III and V of
The Ego and the Id, i.e., . . . "the effects of the first identifications . . . will be . . . lasting"(p. 31).

Comment

In the context of the development of religious ideas,
Freud proposes that helplessness in the child and later in
the adult elicits the adaptive response of turning to the
object for care and protection. He proposes that helplessness in the adult is responsible for the content and form
taken by religious ideas, that these have their prototype in
the dependence of childhood. The helplessness in the adult
perpetuates dependence on the object, and ". . . this time
on a more powerful one . . ." than the actual parent: the
psychic representation of deity (the deity-object representation).

Freud suggests the mechanisms involved in *the image formation of deity*. The mental representation of the archaic parent, overvalued as he appeared to the helpless child, at the behest of helplessness in the adult is displaced onto the image of a deity-object in the representational world which has attributes of that overvalued parent, particularly, in Freud's view, of the father. We would suggest that some of the attributes of the transitional object and of transitional phenomena as formulated by Winnicott (1953), which have found representation in the psyche during the normal symbiotic phase of development, are the source of mystery, omnipotence, vagueness, and so forth, of the qualities ascribed to the deified mental representation. In addition, Freud's assumption that *the origin of belief in deity* lies in the first psychic experience of earliest childhood is discussed in the above references. (See particularly the notes from *Civilization and Its Discontents*.) His descriptions and formulations suggest that the experiences characteristic of the normal symbiotic phase of development (Mahler, 1968b) are nuclear to the *origins of belief in deity*. Freud clearly views both *image formation of deity* and, more important, *the belief in deity* as originating in man's childhood helplessness and dependence on the parents.

3. Dependence and the Resolution of the Oedipus Complex.

When sufficient development of primary autonomous ego function makes awareness of psychologic experience possible, the child's experience of helplessness leads to psychologic dependence on the object. The libidinization of this dependence is the nucleus and source of fear of object-loss and fear of loss of the object's love. Bearing the danger situation series in mind, we turn to Freud's sugges-

tion that the Oedipus complex comes genetically at a time
when the child is too immature to dispense with the "protection, care and indulgence" of his parents (1940, p. 200;
also pp. 184-185). We must, therefore, take cognizance of
the role played by the *then very viable* prephallic determinants of anxiety, in the resolution of the Oedipus complex. Freud did so as early as 1913 when, in *Totem and
Taboo*, he quotes Frazer (1911) in terms of the role the
monarch (father) plays in relation to his subjects (sons):
"The need to protect the king from every possible form of
danger follows from his immense importance to his subjects. . . . The sovereign . . . exists only for his subjects"
(pp. 43-44; see also p. 144). (We will subsequently take up
the role dependence on the object plays in paving the way
for the Oedipus complex.)

Also in *Totem and Taboo* Freud (1913a) points to
the "ambivalence implicit in the father-complex" (p. 145).
Earlier in this work (p. 129) he had stated that the ambivalence toward the father which lies in the boy's hatred and
rivalry with the father for the prime love-object, the mother, comes in opposition to "his old established affection
and admiration" for him. As he will also later observe in
discussing Little Hans (p. 102): "The victory of the son's
affectionate emotions over his hostile ones" (*Totem and
Taboo* [1913a] p. 150) is a component factor leading to
the resolution of the Oedipus complex.

Thus in *Totem and Taboo*, Freud (1913a) elaborates
some of the psychical forces in the dynamics of the father
complex. This is not a statement of all the forces at play in
the dynamics of this complex. The ones to which Freud
here refers consist in: (1) incestual impulses and hostility
toward the father, rival for the love-object; against these
impulses stand (2) the current of affectional libido, "his
old established affection" that retains much of its cathexis

attached to the father and leads to remorse and guilt, and
(3) the dependence on the father "for protection against
the hostile environment, as well as for . . . care and indulgence" (1913a, p. 144). We should observe that points 2
and 3 are the product of libido positions attained prior
to the advent of the phallic phase of psychosexual
development.

In following the thread of man's dependence woven into the fabric of the Oedipus complex and its role in neurosis, we restate several important observations Freud made
in 1926. Neurosis results from the ego's attempt to cope
with its helplessness. Under conditions of helplessness, the
infantile ego, by virtue of its experiences, may turn dependently to the auxiliary ego, the mother, for help. We spoke
earlier of another related development. When Freud suggests that religion saves people from individual neuroses,
he is suggesting that the individual turns to the displaced
archaic parent representation (in the form of Providence)
for protection against helplessness of the ego. Thus, turning dependently to the object, or deity, although it may be
regressive, can save the ego symptom formation.

As we have already stated, Freud in 1926 elaborated the
series of danger situations. First is fear of loss of the anaclitic, symbiotic object which is soon followed by fear of loss
of the love from the object. The danger situation specific
for the phallic phase is castration anxiety. It is followed by
the ego's fear of loss of love from, or punishment by the
super-ego; and, "the final transformation which the fear of
the super-ego undergoes is . . . the fear of death . . . which
is a fear of the super-ego projected on to the powers of
destiny" (p. 140). Indeed, in psychic representational
terms, the archaic object representations that go into super-ego formation are also the ones externalized into deity
image formations.

In examining, then, the role of the determinants of anxiety in neurosis, Freud (1926) states that in phobias, conversion hysteria and obsessional neuroses,

> All three have as their outcome the destruction of the Oedipus complex; and in all three the motive force of the ego's opposition is, we believe, the fear of castration [p. 122]. [Focussing further he questions:] ... is it absolutely certain that fear of castration is the only motive force of repression ...? If we think of neuroses in women, we are bound to doubt it.... [Here] we can hardly speak ... of castration *anxiety* [p. 123; see also p. 142, 143]. [Elsewhere, Freud (1933b) states this most clearly]: Fear of castration is not, of course, the only motive force for repression: Indeed, it finds no place in women, for though they have a castration complex they cannot have a fear of being castrated. Its place is taken in their sex by a *fear of loss of love*, which is ... a later prolongation of the infant's anxiety if it finds its mother absent [p. 87; italics added]. [He had already observed this in 1924 (1924b, p. 178.)]

Freud (1926) introduces a further consideration when he speaks of the phobias of infancy (i.e., unrelenting fear of object loss): "If these early phobias persist ... one is inclined to suspect the presence of a neurotic disturbance, although it is not at all clear what their relation is to the undoubted neuroses that appear later on in childhood" (p. 136).

He throws further light on the subject a few pages later when he remarks that in the evolution of the danger situation series, a later determinant does not invalidate a preceding one; indeed, they "can persist side by side and cause ... anxiety at a period later than the appropriate one" (p. 142).

Freud proposed that in *optimal* development,

> ... certain determinants of anxiety are relinquished and certain danger-situations lose their significance as the individual becomes more mature.... Other determinants of anxiety, [on the other

hand] , such as fear of the superego, are destined not to disappear at all, but to accompany people throughout their lives. . . . A great many people . . . do not overcome determinants of anxiety which have grown out of date. To deny this would be to deny the existence of neurosis for it is precisely such people whom we call neurotics [p. 148] .

The Field of the Oedipus Complex—1926. Bearing these concepts in mind, let us briefly state then the forces at play in the resolution of the pre-latency child's Oedipus complex. From the side of the drives come the incestual impulses and the hostile impulses mobilized by rivalry, which Freud (1913a) pointed out to be the sources of the two prime taboos in totemism: incest and murder. Opposed to the drives stand the anxiety determinants side by side: fear of loss of the object, which more or less gives place to fear of loss of the object's love, fear of castration, specific to the phallic strivings of the boy in his Oedipus complex; and the affectionate current towards the rival love object.

In 1926, Freud cites the relevance of dependence on the parents to the disposition of instinctual drives:

Loss of an object (or loss of love on the part of the object) and the threat of castration are . . . dangers coming from outside. . .; they are not instinctual dangers . . . but the loved person would not cease to love us, nor should we be threatened with castration if we did not entertain certain feelings and intentions within us. Thus such instinctual impulses are determinants of external dangers and so become dangerous in themselves; and we can now proceed against external danger by taking measures against the internal ones [p. 145] .

Or, as he repeats in Addendum B: "We have . . . come to the conclusion that an instinctual demand often only becomes an (internal) danger because its satisfaction would bring on an external danger" (p. 167).

In *An Outline* Freud (1940) expands these issues:
"Children are protected against the dangers . . . from the
external world by . . . their parents; they pay for this security by a fear of *loss of love.* . . . This factor exerts a
decisive influence on the outcome of the conflict when a
boy[3] finds himself in the situation of the oedipus complex, in which the threat . . . of castration . . . takes possession of him" (p. 200).

Comment

In childhood, loss of love is, as is well-known, a frequent, daily occurrence, experienced universally in variable
degrees. As a determinant of anxiety it is ubiquitous, as is
the first determinant of anxiety, dread of loss of the object. Freud has pointed out that the immaturity of the ego
makes it incapable of achieving the aim of the impulses
that emerge with the phallic phase of development; it is
that same immaturity of that same ego that makes the
earlier determinants of anxiety so viable during this phase
of development.

From the assumption prior to 1924-1926 that castration anxiety was the sole determinant of neurosis, Freud
moves to the position that fear of loss of love from the
object in girls and the same fear in addition to fear of
castration in boys lead to repression. He furthermore
noted (1926) that a "neurotic disturbance" is to be sus-
pected in the persistent "phobia of infancy," i.e., in cases
of excessive separation anxiety (p. 136). Inasmuch as the
fear of loss of the object and fear of loss of the object's

[3] Freud had already, from 1924 on, given primacy to fear of loss of love
in the resolution of the Oedipus complex of the girl. Reference to this point
appears in *The Dissolution of the Oedipus Complex,* in *Inhibitions,
Symptoms and Anxiety,* Lectures XXXII and XXXIII, as well as in *An
Outline of Psychoanalysis.*

love are direct derivatives of dependence on the object, contributions to neurosis can be traced to that long childhood dependence.

A view from the epigenetic frame of reference corroborates this thesis: the danger situations specific for earlier periods of development stand side by side with that of castration anxiety in the field of the Oedipus conflict as formulated by Freud. We also find that, alongside these forces leading to the resolution of the Oedipus complex, stands the ". . . old established affection . . ." for the rival parent, an affection derived from the libidinization of the dependence on that object.

One more point arises from the side of reality: who will protect the child against the raging environment if the rage comes from the prime protector himself? The father's love must be retained because of the still existing dependence on him. That is, prephallic determinants of anxiety, still highly viable in the child with an active Oedipus complex exert a powerful influence on the resolution of that complex.

RELATION OF CHILDHOOD DEPENDENCE TO PSYCHIC STRUCTURE FORMATION

We turn now to Freud's formulations of the means by which the characteristics of a child's psychic structure arise out of his relations to his parents. We see, in this context, two interrelated postulates:

1. The initial condition of helplessness of the human infant leads to cathexis of the object. The prime insurer of the gratification of need is love from the object. To retain that love from the object, the infant makes sacrifices, places restrictions on impulse discharge. Thus *the*

love from the parents is a civilizing force that determines, for example, what is repressed, what is right and wrong, thereby affecting in large part the contents and functions of the id, ego and superego. This force is strongest during the earliest years when the child's dependence makes parental approval so important. It is in the context of this thesis, we believe, that in *The Ego and the Id*, Freud remarked that the long period of childhood dependence, together with the resolution of the Oedipus complex, are the two factors that lead to the formation of the superego (1923, p. 35).

2. Freud (1923, 1940) holds that object relations determine the phenotypic expression of our genotypic psychic endowment, to borrow a model from genetics. His formulation of structural theory in 1923 brings into focus the part played by the object, by means of identification and introjection, in the formation of the ego and the superego (Chapters III and V). In this theory, the relation to the love object is the most important factor from the external environment to determine the character of both the child's ego and superego. We refer to what Hartmann (1939) has described as "internalization of the external environment." Thus, we find in Freud's writings the concept that *psychic structure formation is contingent upon object relations*. We turn to Freud's writings.

1. The Role of Parental Love (as Civilizing Force) in Psychic Structure Formation.

Although the theory of psychic structure is formulated for the first time in 1923, Freud's views on the relations of the long childhood dependence to structure formation appear in prior writings.

In *Totem and Taboo* (1913a), speaking of men's relation to the taboos they constructed, Freud observes that "in their unconscious there is nothing they would like more than to violate them" (p. 31). He then states:

> Taboo is a primaeval prohibition forcibly imposed (*by some authority*) *from outside* [p. 34, italics added]. [Therewith, renunciation of the wish is necessary. This is effected by] conscience [which] is the internal perception of the rejection of a particular wish operating within us [p. 68]. [He goes on:] Thus it seems probable that conscience . . . arose on a basis of emotional ambivalence, from . . . *specific human relations* [p. 68, italics added]. The hatred for his father that arises in a boy from rivalry for his mother is not able to achieve uninhibited sway over his mind; it has to contend against the old-established affection and admiration for the very same person [p. 129].

And again, in speaking of the primal horde Freud observed:

> The tumultuous mob of brothers . . . hated their father, . . . but they loved and admired him too. After they had got rid of him, had satisfied their hatred and had put into effect their wish to identify themselves with him, the *affection which had all this time been pushed under* was bound to make itself felt. It did so in the form of remorse. A sense of guilt made its appearance [p. 143, italics added].

Note this early statement on the relations of dependence to superego formation: that the sense of guilt is the result of the unconscious hostile wish encountering the "old-established affection" which we believe arises from the libidinization of the dependence. We see in the above a suggestion that experiencing the affectionate feelings after the hostile wish or act, and not the hostile wish or act per se, leads to remorse. This is an interesting early statement of the dynamics of guilt. Later (1930, 1939), Freud sug-

gests that where sufficient superego formation exists guilt
generally follows hostility per se.

We find a further early thought on superego formation
in "The Claims of Psychoanalysis to Scientific Interest"
(1913b). Noting, as we shall elaborate later, "internalization of the external environment" in individual development, we read: "What is today an act of internal restraint
was once an external one" (p. 189). Shortly before, Freud
(1913a) suggested that the origins of taboo resulted from
the taking into oneself of the "prohibition forcibly imposed (by some authority) from outside" (p. 34). We can
see the soon-to-be-formulated (1923): What was once external restraint is now internalized in the superego. Whereas the ego is the agent of adaptation to psychic life as
Hartmann has elucidated since 1939, we see in Freud's
writings the suggestion that the superego is the agent of
civilization.

Freud's observations suggest that civilization plays a
large part in psychic structure differentiation (1940, p.
185). In "The Claims of Psychoanalysis to Scientific Interest" (1913b), he observes as he did in *Totem and Taboo*
(p. 145-146) that "the whole course of the history of civilization is no more than an account of the various meth-
ods adopted by mankind for 'binding' their unsatisfied
wishes" (p. 186). "*Restriction and repression* of instinct
*owe their origin essentially to compliance with the de-
mands of civilization*" (p. 188, italics added).

In 1927, he comments on man's dependence on the
environment and its relations to the demands of civilization: "little as men are able to exist in isolation they . . .
nevertheless feel as a heavy burden the sacrifices which
civilization expects of them in order to make a communal
life possible" (p. 6). In 1921 he refers to man's anaclitic
social relations: "We are reminded of how many of these

phenomena of dependence are part of the normal constitution of society, . . . of how much every individual is ruled by attitudes of the group mind" (p. 117).

In *Civilization and Its Discontents* (1930), Freud alludes again to man's difficulties in dealing with instinctual impulses (sexual and aggressive now) and the influence of civilization upon these. And again we find: "The word 'civilization' describes the whole sum of the achievements and the regulations . . . which serve two purposes—namely, to protect men against nature and to adjust their mutual relations" (p. 89).

And the fields of civilization are cultivated by the parents, representatives of civilization (1940, p. 185) who, through upbringing, carry out its dictates which influence not only the structuralization of the superego, but of the id and the ego as well.

Love for the Object as Civilizing Force. In 1921, we find a most significant remark: "And in the development of mankind as a whole, just as in individuals, love alone acts as the civilizing factor in the sense that it brings a change from egoism to altruism" (p. 103). Just earlier came the significant "Love for oneself knows only one barrier—love for others, love for objects." (p. 102). This is an economic equation in terms of libido theory. But it is also a genetic and dynamic statement. And so is: "We know that love puts a check upon narcissism and it would be possible to show how, by operating in this way, it became a factor of civilization" (p. 124). Love for the object adds its weight to the side of the forces that lead to the disposition of forbidden impulses as by repression. Thus object love imposes activity by the ego that greatly influences the character of that ego and the contents of the id.

Discussing the origin of the sense of guilt, Freud (1930) states

> We may reject the existence of an original . . . capacity to distinguish good from bad . . . . There is an extraneous influence at work, and it is this that decides what is to be called good or bad. Since a person's own feelings would not have led him along this path, he must have had a motive for submitting to this extraneous influence. *Such a motive is easily discovered in his helplessness and his dependence on other people, and it can best be designated as fear of loss of love.* . . At the beginning, therefore, what is bad is whatever causes one to be threatened with loss of love. . . . At this stage the sense of guilt is clearly only a fear of loss of love [from objects] " (pp. 124-125; italics added).

This concept refers to the superego-precursor stage when the sense of guilt "is the direct derivative of the conflict which is between the need for the authority's love and the urge towards instinctual satisfaction" (p. 136). "A great change takes place only when the authority is internalized through the establishment of a superego" (p. 125). The ego then becomes, in a sense, dependent for love on the superego; however, by this internalization, the child becomes more self-reliant. Thereby, internalization of parental authority into the superego, which significantly decreases man's dependence on an actual object for love and regulation of impulses, serves "the process of civilization" (p. 140).

Of course, the latency-age child and even the adolescent are still dependent on parental love and authority after superego structuralization. And indeed, many an adult (to stay for a moment with the anthropomorphic model), when the superego fails to support him, again seeks an external authority in Fate. Even in adults, a certain complementary economic relationship exists between love from the superego and the need for love and protection from the external objects or object substitutes.

Lack of Love and Ego-Ideal. In 1933, Freud notes that lack of parental love leads to feelings of inferiority: "A child feels inferior if he notices that he is not loved; and so does an adult" (p. 65). (See also pp. 20-21, in *Beyond the Pleasure Principle.*) Freud (1933a) ties the sense of inferiority to the withdrawal of love from the mother—which we know from 1914 would lead to a lowering of self-esteem. These notes point to the relation of dependence for love on objects to the status of self-esteem and thereby to ego-ideal.

Our notes on this thesis end here. We do not claim originality for Freud in unfolding his postulate that the long dependence of the child on his parents has its great share in civilizing him. Original, however, is the fact that Freud's remarks are made in terms of psychic structure formation; and we find it to be an impressively recurrent motif. The thesis holds that the dependence on the parents and the resolution of the Oedipus complex greatly influence the character of psychic structure formation. We have recorded here some of the references he made to the contributions deriving from the dependence on the object; we find frequent reference to parental love as a civilizing factor. And of course, Freud repeatedly observed that the dictates of civilization, carried out by the parents, determine to a large extent what is repressed, the development of morality and ideals, modes of adaptation, and thus, in short, the character of the id, ego, and superego.

2. Dependence—Object-Cathexis—Identification—Structure Formation

We turn now to the second postulate, one which is both rich and complex. One of the great influences dependence on the object has upon psychic structure formation comes from the assimilative processes, identification and introjection. We admit to being free in our use of the term identification; it is our impression (and that of others) that this term had not been rigorously defined by Freud. We are, in fact, alluding to the generic process of assimilation of external environment into psychic organization which we now know to be complex and to consist of more than processes of identification and introjection—a theory to which Freud called attention in 1923. We speak of Hartmann's (1939) "internalization of the external environment" as we follow the thread: dependence (object cathexis)—identification—structure formation.

The Ego and the Id (1923) is a monument in psychoanalysis. Here (also in Lecture XXXI, p. 66 and in *An Outline of Psychoanalysis*, p. 146 and 205) Freud cites two factors that lead to the formation of the superego: (1) the long period of childhood dependence and, (2) the resolution of the Oedipus complex (p. 35). He went further in *An Outline of Psychoanalysis*, venturing that indeed any organism which, like man, has a protracted phase of helplessness and dependence in its childhood probably develops a superego (1940, p. 147). Our interest here lies not in whether nonhuman animals have a superego, but in Freud's view of the great genetic influence which helplessness and dependence have on psychic structure formation. Freud states this explicitly in *The Ego and the Id.* Let us examine his remarks in some detail.

Before picking up the thread of dependence—identification—structure formation at the time structural theory was elaborated, we trace some of Freud's earlier remarks on the assimilative processes relevant to our present focus.

Identification Prior To 1923. Among the earliest (1909) comments pointing to identification we note from "Family Romances," p. 237: "For a small child his parents are at first the only authority and the source of all belief. The child's most intense and most momentous wish during these early years is to be like his parents (that is, the parent of his own sex) and to be big like his father and mother." This wish is gratified through identification, described as an oral process in *Totem and Taboo* (1913a) ". . . in the act of devouring him [the totem animal, the father] they accomplished their identification with him and . . . acquired a portion of his strength" (p. 142). The process of identification as described in "Mourning and Melancholia" again assigns this mechanism to the period of maximal dependence on the object: the oral phase.

But, in "Mourning and Melancholia" the question of identification takes a most remarkable turn. Freud states (1917a) that, in melancholia, upon loss (actual or fantasied) of the object, "The object-cathexis proves to have little power of resistance . . . [and its libido, detaching from the object is] withdrawn into the ego . . . [where it establishes] an *identification* of the ego with the abandoned object" (p. 249). He points out that it is the ego, not "the critical activity of the ego" (i.e., the future superego) that is altered by this "regressive" identification. And he adds: "The narcissistic identification with the object then becomes a substitute for the erotic cathexis, the result of which is *that the love-relation need not be given up*" (p. 249, italics added). Thus we can say that with loss of the object dependence on the object is given up only in external reality, *but not intrapsychically*.

In this work, Freud described the framework for the concept that an actual, highly-cathected object can be given up only by internalizing the object relation, whereupon "the shadow of the object" falls upon the ego. The lost object is "taken into" structure and modifies that structure's character, i.e., its contents and functions. This ap-

plies both to the ego and the superego. Although this remarkable theory, that *an object cathexis is replaced by an
identification and thereby modifies structure,* has its origin
in the study of melancholia, Freud later (1923) generalized
it as a normative process which pertains to both ego and
superego formation.

In 1921, Freud takes a further step in clarifying the
relations of object cathexis and identification. In *Group
Psychology and the Analysis of the Ego* he notes for the
first time that identification precedes object cathexis and
is distinct from it. This is first suggested here (p. 105) and
is considered to be so by Freud thereafter. This reference
is to "primary identification" upon which, as is well
known, he did not significantly elaborate. (See below, *The
Ego and the Id.*)

We find that references to identification in *Group
Psychology and the Analysis of the Ego* are particularly
relevant to the character of the object relations established
with the parents during the first two or so years of life.
Freud (1921) states that "Identification is . . . the earliest
expression of an emotional tie with another person." And
suggesting prephallic phase developments: "A little boy
will exhibit a special interest in his father; he would like to
grow like him and be like him, and take his place everywhere" (p. 105).

In summarizing his observations on identification in
1921, Freud makes several points:

> First, identification is the original form of emotional tie with an
> object; secondly, in a regressive way it becomes a substitute for a
> libidinal object-tie, as it were by means of introjection of the
> object into the ego; and thirdly, it may arise with any new percep-
> tion of a common quality shared with some other person [p.
> 107-108].

Still referring to processes of identification and introjection and in discussing the splitting off of the "ego ideal" (superego) from the ego, he says: "[the superego] has revealed its origin in the influence of superior powers, and above all of parents" (p. 110). Here Freud already had evolved concepts basic to the formulation of the superego, already suggesting the core of the superego to be the identifications with the parents. He concludes with a question that hints at Chapters III and V of *The Ego and the Id*, and is most relevant to the point we wish to make. Freud's question: "*Whether* [in identification] *the object is put in the place of the ego or of the ego-ideal*" (p. 114). We ask a less difficult question: How relevant are the love objects to the structuralization of each, the ego and the superego?

Identification: 1923 and After. Before answering our question we must clarify an aspect of structural development. We note that Freud (1923) postulates not only a *functional* construct of the id, ego, and superego here, but a *structural* construct. He states that ". . . all knowledge has its origin in external perceptions" (p. 23). We assume that "external" means external to the psyche, to the mind. Thus proprioceptive, enteroceptive and nociceptive stimuli are obviously external to the perceptual apparatus of the central nervous system. This point is important for concepts of the psychic internal representational world. The ego "starts. . .from the system *Pcpt.*,[4] which is its nucleus, and begins by embracing the *Pcs.*, which is adjacent to the mnemic residues." And the ego then extends into the id "which behaves as though it were *Ucs*" (p. 23). He continues, looking on the individual as a "psychical id, unknown

[4] Pcpt.= The perceptual system of the psychic apparatus. See Freud, 1900, pp. 536-549. Pcs.= The preconscious.

and unconscious, upon whose surface rests the ego, developed from its nucleus the *Pcpt.* system" (p. 24).

The ego then (and the id), as Hartmann has now extensively elaborated, has its origins in man's biological adaptational systems, and has primary autonomous apparatuses. Thus, as far as the id and the ego are concerned, the influences of the environment act upon genotypic anlage that will allow for a myriad, but not an infinite, number of potential phenotypic expressions. Freud observes that the superego on the other hand, differentiates from this biopsychologic ego *solely* as the result of the experiences in the environment. He never deviates from this view. He asserts that the superego is in origin a psychical construct, in important measure the result of man's long childhood helplessness and dependence on the environment. By what means does this superego develop and what is the relevance of helplessness and dependence to its development? The same may be asked of the ego, although we must today bear in mind the presence of constitutional anlage in the ego. Back to dependence–identification–structure formation.

In *The Ego and the Id* Freud further advances the theory in focus here:

> In melancholia an object which was lost has been set up again inside the ego—that is, . . . an object-cathexis has been replaced by an identification. . . . *[T]his kind of substitution has a great share in determining the form taken by the ego and . . . it makes an essential contribution towards building up . . . its 'character' "* [p. 28; italics added] .

From the vicissitudes of the object cathexis in melancholia, Freud turns to the vicissitudes of object cathexis in normal development:

It may be that this identification [introjection] *is the sole condition under which the id can give up its objects.* . . . [T] he process, especially in the early phases of development, is a very frequent one, and it makes it possible to suppose that *the character of the ego is a precipitate of abandoned object-cathexes* [p. 29; italics added].

Thus the object cathexes, particularly in early development, shape the ego in content and function. Therefore, we say that the structuring of the ego is anaclitic; object relations are essential for optimal ego development.

It remained for Freud (1923) to state that an object cathexis is transformed into an identification even in cases where the actual object is not lost or given up. Indeed, he adds:

We must also take into consideration cases of simultaneous object-cathexis and identification—cases, that is, in which the alteration in character occurs before the object has been given up. In such case the alteration in character [of the ego] has been able to survive the object-relation and in a certain sense to conserve it [pp. 29-30].

The question may arise in the reader's mind: if an object is not given up, how then can an identification occur? Just before, we quoted Freud to have said of identification: ". . . [T] he process especially in the early phase of development, is a very frequent one" (p. 29). The above statements leave no room for doubt that what is given up is an object cathexis, not the object or the object relation, and that any one significant object relation is based on a series of cathexes of the same object from more archaic to recent and current cathexis bindings. Freud's theory of mourning supports this assumption. He tells us (1917a) that the detachment of the libido from the lost object reveals this object libido to consist of a series of object cathexes that have to be worked through one by one. He states that the love-object representation

> ... is made of innumerable single impressions (or unconscious traces of them) and this withdrawal of libido is ... a process ... in which progress is long-drawn-out and gradual. . . . [I] n analysis it often becomes evident that first one and then another memory is activated, and that the laments which always sound the same ... nevertheless take their rise each time in some different unconscious source [p. 256].

In *The Ego and the Id* he adds yet another link to the theory, a fascinating transformation of energy into structure: "[The ego] withdraws libido from the id and transforms the object-cathexis of the id into ego-structures" (p. 55). We have not found in our studies of Freud's writings, how the energic to structural transformation occurs. And we leave this question here.

We pause to present a simplified diagram of this most important theory:

Dependence on the object for
object cathexes
↓
Identification
↓
Psychic structure formation,
Progressive modification

Freud (1923) then turns to the basically common *psychic* origins of both the ego and the superego. He comments on the genetic aspects of the earliest object relations:

> "But, whatever the character's later capacity for resisting the influences of abandoned object-cathexes ... the effects of the first

identifications made in earliest childhood will be general and lasting. This leads us back to the origin of the ego ideal [superego];
for behind it there lies hidden an individual's first and most important identification, his identification with ... the parents" [see
p. 31, Footnote No. 1]. This is apparently not in the first instance
the consequence or outcome of an object-cathexis; it is a direct
and immediate identification and takes place earlier than any object-cathexis [p. 31] [primary identification]. But the object-
choices belonging to the first sexual period and relating to the
father and mother seem normally to find their outcome in an
identification of this kind [secondary identification] and would
thus reinforce the primary one [p. 31].

The superego differentiates from the ego by the forming
of a precipitate of both the primary identifications with
the parents and the secondary ones associated with the
resolution of the oedipus complex.

> The superego is, however, not simply a residue of the earliest
> object-choices of the id; it also represents an energetic reaction-
> formation against those choices [p. 34].

In Chapter V, Freud summarizes:

> ... *the ego is formed to a great extent out of identifications* which
> *take the place of abandoned cathexes* by the id; [and] the first of
> these identifications ... stand apart from the ego in the form of a
> super-ego.... *It is a memorial of the former weakness and depen-*
> *dence of the ego*, and the mature ego remains subject to its domi-
> nation. As the child was once under a compulsion to obey its
> parents, so the ego submits to the categorical imperative of its
> super-ego [p. 48; italics added].

Here as in 1917 (p. 242), Freud asserts that the superego originates from and owes its existence to identifications. The ego, on the other hand, has a primary biologic
origin with physiologic anlage, but, as Freud impressively
delineated it in 1923, we cannot underestimate the significance of the cathexis of objects and of the assimilative
processes for its eventual structuralization. And it is exact-

ly *the libidinization of the dependence on the specific objects that insures that a given child's psychic structure will
be molded by the internalization of the experiences with
his particular parents.* In this sense, psychic structure formation is anaclitic.

Later Freud (1933) again comments on primary and
secondary identifications in the process of superego structuralization:

> In the course of development the superego also takes on the
> influences of those who have stepped into the place of parents—
> educators, teachers, people chosen as ideal models. Normally it
> departs more and more from the original parental figures. . . . Nor
> must it be forgotten that a child has a different estimate of its
> parents at different periods of its life. At the time at which the
> Oedipus complex gives place to the super-ego, they are something
> quite magnificent; but later they lose much of this. Identifications
> then come about with these later parents as well, and indeed they
> *regularly make important contributions to the formation of char-*
> *acter* [also see p. 91]; *but in that case they only affect the ego,*
> *they no longer influence the super-ego* which has been determined
> by the earliest parental imago [pp. 63-64; italics added].

(See "The Economic Problem of Masochism," 1924a, p.
168). We do not understand why Freud suggests this im-
munity-to-change of the superego; its structuralization
with the resolution of the Oedipus complex does not require subsequent fixity. Consideration of the Principle of
Multiple Function (Waelder, 1930) requires greater clarification of the statement that there exists a very different
susceptibility to change for the superego as compared with
the ego. Waelder (1937) wrote that the superego is modifiable even in the third decade of life. Much remains to be
understood to date on this point. We leave this major thread:
dependence (object-cathexis)—identification—structure formation, a most critical hypothesis for psychoanalytic devel-

opmental psychology. In it, the bridge between object relations and structure formation is lucidly drawn, albeit it is un-
finished in detail.

We close with quotations from Freud's final magnum
opus. In *An Outline of Psychoanalysis* (1940) regarding
the behavior of the libido, he states: "A characteristic of
the libido which is important in life is its *mobility*, the
facility with which it passes from one object to another.
This must be contrasted with the *fixation* of the libido to
particular objects, which often persists throughout life" (p.
151; our italics). No one, we believe, escapes some such
fixation of libido upon representations of the first anaclitic
objects, the parents, with the resultant establishment of
these representations in the basic character of the ego and
the superego, as well as in identity formations.

In a most succinct description of the global functions of
psychic structure, Freud says, of the id:

> This oldest portion of the psychical apparatus remains the most
> important throughout life [p. 145].... The power of the id ex-
> presses the true purpose of the individual organism's life. This
> consists in *the satisfaction of its innate needs....* [It] is the task
> of the ego ... to discover the most favorable and least perilous
> method of obtaining satisfaction, *taking the external world into
> account.* The super-ego may bring fresh needs to the fore, but its
> main function remains the limitation of satisfactions [p. 148;
> italics added].

The psychic apparatus is surely, as Freud asserts, "developed by the exigencies of life" (p. 196).

We focus for another moment on id processes *vis-à-vis*
need satisfaction and the relations of objects to both

> The one and only urge of [the] instincts is towards satisfac-
> tion, which is expected to arise from certain changes in the organs
> *with the help of objects in the external world.* But immediate

unheeding satisfaction of the instincts, such as the id demands, would often lead to perilous *conflicts with the external world* and to extinction [1940, p. 198; italics added]. [It follows that] experience may have taught the ego that the satisfaction of some instinctual demand ... would involve dangers in the external world, so that an instinctual demand of that kind itself becomes a danger [pp. 199-200].

Thus, the objects—and progressively, the ego—mediate between satisfaction and repression, thereby influencing psychic structure formation.

Freud also says (1940):

[The ego] ... *in the persistence with which it maintains its dependence on the external world,* ... *bears the indelible stamp of its origin* (as it might be 'Made in Germany') [p. 199; italics added]... We have repeatedly had to insist on the fact that the ego owes its origin as well as the most important of its acquired characteristics to its relation to the real external world [p. 201].

In the last brief chapter of *An Outline*, Freud says of the superego at approximately age five:

A portion of the external world has, at least partially, been abandoned as an object and has instead, by identification, been taken into the ego and thus become an integral part of the internal world. This new psychical agency continues to carry on the functions which have hitherto been performed by the people ... in the external world: it observes the ego, gives it orders, judges it and threatens it with punishments, exactly like the parents whose place it has taken [p. 205].

Many of those functions which the parents carried out for the child, he asserts, also are internalized and taken over, however, by the ego. Such functions as patterns of reality testing, relating to objects, control and expression of in-

stinctual drives, autonomous ego activity, defenses—as ex-
emplified in the parents' behavior—are internalized and assimilated into structure.

Comment

Freud frequently refers to the influence of the child's
dependence on the development of his psychic structure.
In two senses dependence on the object leads to developments in psychic structure formation:

1. The child becomes civilized to retain love from the
objects on whom he depends for survival. As early as 1913,
parental dictates were said to be internalized due to the
continued need for "care, protection and indulgence" by
the parents. Love and the need for love and protection,
along with fear of punishment, lead to activity by the ego
(as repression) that influences both its characteristic patterns of functioning as well as the character of the (repressed) contents of the id. With the later (1933) formulations
of the ego-ideal, Freud observes that lack of parental love
leads to feelings of inferiority and that the character of the
earliest object relations profoundly influences self-concepts, actual and ideal.

2. Object relations play an indispensible part in psychic
structure formation. In *The Ego and the Id*, Freud under-
scored the hypothesis that it is by the assimilations of the
earliest object relations into the psychic organization that
the ego and the superego develop in man as they do; as
Hartmann suggested in 1939, it is by the internalization of
the external environment. We may note here as Hartmann
observed (1939, p. 40), that it is by this internalization
that the original dependence is largely converted into self-
reliance. The cathexes of the love objects during the first

years of life are intense. These cathexes, arising largely out of the experiences of dependence on the object, can be given up only by a substitutive identification with the object. Freud subsequently added that especially in early life, identification with the object occurs simultaneously with the ongoing object relation as the cathexis undergoes modification and detachment from earlier object representations. The cathexis and the object representation are taken into the ego and superego by identification, and thereby a modification of that ego and superego occurs.

There is little doubt that identifications arise from the need to retain the psychic relation to the object. The importance of the relation to the object and the valuation of the object have their origin in the condition of helplessness and dependence of the child. It is exactly the libidinization of dependence on the specific objects which insures that a child's psychic structure will be molded by the internalization of experiences with his parents. If the child were not bound to the object through its psychologic dependence upon it, if the cathexis of that object were not powerful, the object could be given up with little consequence to psychic structure, since no identification would occur.

DEPENDENCE AND THE TWO CURRENTS OF THE LIBIDO

The experiences of frustration and gratification lead to valuation of the object; its mental representations become cathected with libido. What kind of libido? Sensual libido? Affectional libido? Alloys of the two? (We shall not concern ourselves here with aggression.)

As early as 1905 Freud suggested that the libido consisted of two currents, the affectionate and the sexual (sensual). Because his views on this concept may carry implications not only for the further development of libido theory but for neurosis and human development in general, we trace them here. We find also that the concept of two currents of the libido highlights the role dependence plays in libido theory. Although we hear little of dependence in libido theory, it appears repeatedly in Freud's writings.

As we follow a chronologic sequence in the evolving of Freud's thoughts, we ask the reader to bear two foci in mind. First, we trace the vicissitudes of the dichotomy "affectional and sensual components of libido"[5] in Freud's writings, noting that the affectional object-libido precedes sensual object-libido in its emergence. Second, we draw attention to the importance of the affectional current for the attachment of the sensual current to the love object; in other words, the affectional current paves the way for the oedipus complex. Freud observed, and ethological studies (Lorenz, Hess and others, see Chapter 2) support the hypothesis that the libidinization of the object with anaclitic affectional libido *leads* to the attachment of phallic, sensual cathexes to that object.

We do not propose that the dichotomy of affectional and sensual libido is a simple matter. For example, although erotism is understood to be anaclitic, to lean upon physiologic function (as erotism of the oral mucosa is assumed to be activated at the outset of extrauterine life, by the physiologic function of sucking), both occur very early in life, well before libidinization of the object takes place. As psychic experience, oral erotism antedates any affectional current of libido. How can we then say that sensual libido, of which oral and anal erotism are early differentiations, *follows* affectional libido? We can say that only if

[5]Clinically this dichotomy may be useful. How often we agree that a given patient's genital behavior is less genital than "oral-dependent;" or that, in other cases, the latter is a defense against the former. Empirically we know that such a dichotomy can narrow or broaden one's perspective. Our hope is to obtain the latter.

we speak, not of erotism (i.e., *auto*erotism), but of *object*
libido. It is exactly in the area of object libido that we can
say that, in normal development, affectional libido makes
the path for genital libido. Let us trace these developments
in Freud's writings.

The Affectional and Sensual Valuations—Pre-1914

Prior to 1914, the problem of a dichotomy of affectionate and sexual[6] currents was readily solvable: instinct theory of the period was not unfavorable to such a dichotomy
of libido—the affectional valuations were made by the ego
(self-preservative) instincts (1912, p. 181); the sensual ones
then by the sexual instincts.

In 1912 Freud states that the "affectionate current is
the older of the two" (p. 180) and "the sexual instincts
find their first objects by attaching themselves to the *valuations made by the ego instincts*" (p. 181; italics added).

Freud suggests a complication in the character and origin of the affectional current. In the *Three Essays* he notes
that with latency, repression of sexual aims occurs with
the emergence of the affectional current (1905, p. 200).
He informs us, however, that he is referring to the phallic
phase of psychosexual development, between "the ages of
two and five", which is characterized by the emergence of
genital (phallic) sexual libido. The two years preceding this
development did not then claim Freud's attention.

---

[6] For the sake of internal consistency we will use the term "affectional"
rather than "affectionate," and "sensual" rather than "sexual," where sexual
is intended in the narrow sense in which Freud used it before 1920 (*Beyond
the Pleasure Principle*). The term "affectional," which we prefer to "affectionate" was used by Harlow et al. (1959, 1960, 1966) in object-relations
theory, however, we do not intend the global meaning of "affectional behavior" conveyed to us by Harlow's usage. We speak of libido, not behavior.

The complication to which we refer is the assumption that, first, an affectional current *precedes* the phallic, sensual cathexis; and second, an affectional current emerges in association with the repression of sexual aims of that period (the phallic phase), i.e., *following* the first genital sensual cathexis. It would appear then, that the first type of affectional cathexis attaches to need satisfaction on a dyadic model of object relations. The second type of affectional cathexis, which emerges in a triadic object relation, does not lead to an additional amount of an anaclitic type of affectional libido—rather it modifies the existing affectional libido, on the basis of the following developments.

The nearly total dependence of the first year of life has been replaced to a significant degree during the phallic phase by internalized constructs, by object and self constancy, identity formations, and individuation which make the child less helpless and less than totally dependent on the anaclitic object. The modification of phallic-phase affectional libido, is, in part, the result of these changes in psychic constructs: and this modification is also influenced by the sensual cathexes and their sublimations into secondary affectional cathexes and altruism.

Although we do not want to complicate issues, we are forced to suggest primary and secondary affectional cathexes, as we perceive the vicissitudes of the affectional current differentiating epigenetically. For example, in *Totem and Taboo*, while tracing the origin of taboo in the father-complex, Freud draws attention to the boy's "old established affection" for his father. He states that this affection, derived from the earliest experiences of helplessness and dependence, *precedes the emergence of the father complex*, and that, as we quoted earlier (1913a), "after [the sons] had satisfied their hatred ... the affection *which had all this time been pushed under* was bound to make itself felt" (p. 143; italics added). The source of hate referred to here is, of course, rivalry with the father for sole possession of the mother.

The thread of two currents of libido emerges again in the metapsychological papers. The editors of the *Standard Edition* give as one of the reasons they consider "On Narcissism" (1914) "among the most important of Freud's writings", that "it enters into the deeper problems of the relations between the ego and the external objects" (p. 70). For just that reason it is of particular interest to us here. In "On Narcissism," Freud ventures "to touch on the question of what makes it necessary at all for our mental life to pass beyond the limits of narcissism and to attach the libido to objects" (p. 85). For a discussion of this question we take a brief detour on the recommendation of the editors, who refer us to "Instincts and Their Vicissitudes" (1915). There, in a footnote on p. 134, we find one answer:

> Those sexual instincts *which from the outset require an object*, and the needs of the ego instincts, *which are never capable of auto-erotic satisfaction*, naturally disturb this state [of primal narcissim] and so pave the way for an advance from it. Indeed, the primal narcissistic state would not be able to follow the development ... if it were not for the fact that every individual passes through a period during which is he helpless ... and during which his pressing needs are satisfied by an external agency and thus are prevented from becoming greater [italics added].

The editors refer to these instinct groupings as "auto-erotic libidinal instincts" and "*non*auto-erotic libidinal instincts" which, along with the self-preservative (ego) instincts, are dependent upon the object for satisfaction (p. 134 to 135).

We return now to the opus of 1914 where Freud again suggests that the libido (sexual instincts) becomes attached to the need-satisfying object (see also 1905, p. 222):

> The first autoerotic sexual satisfactions are experienced in con-
> nection with vital functions which serve the purpose of self-pre-
> servation. The sexual instincts are at the onset attached to the
> satisfaction of the ego instincts; only later do they become inde-
> pendent of these, and even then we have an indication of that
> original attachment in the fact that the persons who are concern-
> ed with a child's feeding, care, and protection become his earliest
> sexual objects: that is to say, . . . his mother [p. 87].

This complex statement led the editors to point out that "the 'attachment'. . . indicated by the term is that of the sexual instincts to the ego instincts, not of the child to its mother" (Footnote 2, p. 87). The issue is complicated by the fact that Freud here speaks of *object choice* of the "anaclitic or attachment type." The editors alert us that Freud does not speak of child to mother dependent behavior as being anaclitic; the narcissist is as dependent on the object as anyone else—and the narcissistic object choice is at the opposite pole from the anaclitic object choice.

We see that Freud's use of the term "attachment" pertains to the relationship of sexual to ego instincts. Subsequently, however, the term seems to refer to the type of object choice made according to the attachment of the libido to self or to the object, as in Freud's summary of

> the paths leading to the choice of an object. The person may
> love:—(1) According to the narcissistic type: . . . what he himself
> is, . . . was, . . . [or] would like to be [or] someone who was once
> part of himself. (2) According to the anaclitic (attachment) type:
> . . . the woman who feeds him, . . . the man who protects him,
> and the succession of substitutes who take their place [p. 90].

We see in Freud's reference from p. 87 two anaclitic
relationships: (1) The sexual instincts follow the self-preservative instincts—as oral erotism follows upon the physiologic sucking reflex; and (2) The persons who libidinally
care for the child become his earliest sexual objects. We see
two further anaclitic relations in this second point: (a) The
infant attaches primary affectional cathexis to the object
who gratifies the "non-autoerotic libidinal" and "self-preservative" needs, i.e., primary affectional cathexes follow
from need gratification; and (b) The earliest object-directed sexual instincts are attached to the object that is libidinized with primary affectional cathexis, i.e., the first object-directed sexual cathexis leans upon the primary affectional cathexis.

Several questions that lead to modification in instinct
theory are raised in the paper, "On Narcissism." They relate (1) to the locus of attachment of libido, i. e., narcissistic versus object; and (2) to the character of instinct: sexual versus ego instinct. As a result of this transition in libido
theory, we seem to lose the dichotomy in libido, and indeed, in a brief digression, Freud questioned if there might
not be "a single kind of psychical energy" (1914, p. 76).
This postulate, however, according to his editors would
create problems since it would not allow the existence of
"ego-interests or simply 'interest' . . . regularly contrasted
with 'libido,' . . . [albeit] the exact nature of these nonlibidinal instincts was obscure" (1915, p. 115). Regretta-
bly this has not been clarified to date. We do not believe
the dichotomy of libido and aggression resolves the question of "ego-interests." Such clarification would be of
great value.

In "Instincts and Their Vicissitudes," (1915) Freud extends our understanding of the character of attachment to
the object as he attempts to clarify the development of
love: "We should prefer to regard loving as the expression

of the *whole* sexual current of feeling . . ." (p. 133). We believe that with this statement he moves towards redefining Eros to the broader meaning it will acquire in *Beyond the Pleasure Principle,* in *Group Psychology,* and thereafter. Originally, he points out (1915):

> . . . the external world is not cathected with interest (in a general sense) and is indifferent for purposes of satisfaction . . . . *The object is brought to the ego from the external world* in the first instance *by the instincts of self-preservation.* . . . If the object becomes a source of pleasurable feelings, a motor urge is set up which seeks to bring the object closer to the ego and to incorporate it into the ego. We then speak of the 'attraction' exercised by the pleasure-giving object and say that we 'love' that object. Conversely, if the object is a source of unpleasurable feelings, . . . [w]e feel the 'repulsion' of the object and hate it [pp. 134-137; italics added].

Freud (1915) then elaborates evolving characteristics of loving. He reflects first on what we have termed the libidinization of dependence: "We do not say of objects which serve the interests of self-preservation that we *love* them; we emphasize the fact that we *need* them, and perhaps express an additional, different kind of relation to them by using words that denote a much reduced degree of love— such as, for example, 'being fond of', 'liking' or 'finding agreeable' " (p. 137). We believe that when Freud speaks of a "much reduced degree of love" he refers to the *quality* of feeling experience toward the need-satisfying object. The degree to which the needed object is longed for by the dependent child can be as intense as is the intensity with which the sexually loved object is longed for. In (1915) Freud observes that

> . . . the word "to love" moves . . . further and further into the sphere of the pure pleasure-relation of the ego to the object and finally becomes fixed to sexual objects in the narrower sense and

to those which satisfy the need of sublimated sexual instincts [p. 137]. [As Freud defines it,] the word "love" can only begin to be applied in this relation [of the ego to the sexual object] after there has been a synthesis of all the component instincts of sexuality under the primacy of the genitals and in the service of the reproductive function [pp. 137-138].

Thus we understand that love, "as the expression of the *whole* sexual current of feeling," includes a quality of libido arising from the earliest experiences of need-satisfaction subsequently combined with a quality of libido arising from sensual impulses. In order for the character of the cathexis to be identifiable as love in Freud's use of the term, we must take into account a time factor: the sensual (genital) impulses become object-directed, essentially with the advent of the phallic phase of psychosexual development.

We have attempted to cite passages relevant to dependence and to the currents of libido—as we see them during this transitional period in instinct theory. We have encountered difficulties inherent in these constructs, but also much clarity and usefulness. We see in these formulations, particularly in "Instincts and Their Vicissitudes," that the continuum of object love represents an epigenesis of cathectic states (1915, p. 137) as follows:

1. Infantile narcissism (primary narcissism) is characterized by indifference to the object.[7]

---

[7]With reference to this earliest stage of the differentiation of libido, we note that Abraham proposed a schema of stages of object-love that seems to correspond with recent formulations of development by Mahler, Jacobson, and Spitz. Abraham (1924, p. 496) outlined the following schema (we have not included his phallic-genital phase which is classical and we have reversed the order of his presentation):

Stages of Libidinal Organization	Stages of Object-Love
1. Earlier Oral Stage (sucking)	1. *Auto-erotism* (without object)
2. Later Oral Stage (cannibalistic)	2. *Narcissism* (total incorporation of object)
3. Earlier Anal-sadistic stage	3. Partial love with incorporation
4. Later Anal-sadistic stage	4. Partial love

2. The earliest stage of object love coincides with cathecting with "interest" the object who gratifies needs, libidinal and ego-instinctual (1915, pp. 134-135). This seems consonant with the appearance of what Freud had called the "affectionate current" (1912, p. 180); the primary condition for the emergence of affectional libido in the human child is satisfaction of anaclitic needs.

3. With the phallic phase, the sensual current becomes object-directed and follows the path to the object already traced by the affectional (anaclitic) cathexis (1914, p. 87). The combination of the affectional and the sensual currents satisfies Freud's term "love".

4. With the necessity for repressing the sensual impulses toward the parental love-object, the sensual libido is, in part, transformed into altruistic affectional libido; by this transformation the pregenital affectional libido is further modified in the direction of altruism.

5. With the mature genital organization, beyond puberty, the combination of affectional and sensual currents differs by two factors from the combination that presented during the phallic phase of psychosexual development:

    a. The psychic organism is more mature in its totality; and,

---

1. The stage of nondifferentiation (Spitz, 1965b) of self and object—coinciding with Freud's (1940), Hartmann's (1939, 1952) undifferentiated id-ego state and (1946) Mahler's normal autistic phase (1968b). This extends from birth to about two months. Mahler's term seems to correlate with Abraham's "(without object.)"

2. The stage of infantile narcissism (Jacobson raises question, 1954, 1964)—coinciding with the first part of Mahler's normal symbiotic phase. The smiling response is a good landmark for its beginning. This would be earlier than the "later oral stage" of Abraham. But the term "symbiosis" connotes Abraham's "total incorporation of object," the object held within the symbiotic membrane (Mahler).

3. Would correspond to No. 2 in the text. It would coincide with the beginning of Mahler's separation-individuation phase starting at about five or six months, at the peak of the symbiosis. Separation anxiety signified its beginning. The object has been libidinized, i.e., object love has its beginnings here. The object relation is profoundly anaclitic.

b. The character of the affectional current is
now dominated by its altruistic character rather
than its anaclitic character. This includes a significant further shift in libido with regard to the
object, from self as object to love-object as object. Thus the shift is from "to get" to "to give"
(Saul, 1947), and from passivity to activity.

Reformulation of Libido—1920

When Freud thought of the sexual and the ego instincts
as separate, one could easily hold to a separation of the
affectional current arising from valuations made by the ego
instincts and sensual current arising from the valuations
made by the sexual instincts. But with the reformulation
of libido theory in 1920, this dichotomy was semantically
less tenable. Eros, as is well-known, was then redefined in
broader terms—as the instinctual unification of two bodies,
two cells, and now included the self-preservative (ego) and
sexual instincts (1920, Chapter VI; 1921, p. 90). In *Group
Psychology*, and later in *Civilization and Its Discontents*,
there is no doubt that the dichotomy of affectional and
sensual libido is swallowed up into the sexual instincts. We
will gain the theory of aggression from this change, a theory of great importance; but in terms of libido, some clarity
is lost. What seems to remain from this merger are the
secondary affectional cathexes, which result from the sublimation of sexual cathexes. This suggests that affectional
libido is only the product of sublimation. With regard to
"love," Freud (1921) now states, "The nucleus of what we
mean by love ... consists ... in sexual love with sexual
union as its aim. But we do not separate from this ...
self-love ... love for parents and children, friendship and

love for humanity in general, and also devotion to concrete objects and to abstract ideas" (p. 90).

Yet the difficulties of semantics here do not change the subsequently oft-repeated postulate of what we call the libidinization of the dependence: "The libido attaches itself to the satisfaction of the great vital needs, and chooses as its first objects, the people who have a share in that process" (1921, p. 103. He repeats this in 1927, p. 24 and in 1933, p. 118). And again, in *Inhibitions, Symptoms and Anxiety* (1926): "At birth no object existed. . . . Since then repeated situations of satisfaction have created an object out of the mother; and this object, whenever the infant feels a need, receives an intense cathexis which might be described as a 'longing' one" (p. 170). As Freud spells out in the danger situation series, this longing bespeaks the dependence on the mother, first in terms of fear of loss of the object, and second, in fear of loss of the object's love. When we push some of the complexities of this issue out of the way, we see that with the unification of ego and sexual instincts the dependence on the object arises from the *nonautoerotic libidinal instincts*, which, by their character enforce object cathexes, i.e., they require the object for gratification. Thus, whereas oral and anal erotism (which are principally autoerotic) negatively determine the distribution of object-libido, the dependence on the object (necessitated by *nonautoerotic* libidinal instincts) positively determines the distribution of object libido. We are referring to the reversible equation, first elaborated by Freud in the paper "On Narcissism," regarding the status of the narcissistic and object libido: narcissistic libido/object libido. (See also *Group Psychology and the Analysis of the Ego*, p. 102: "love for oneself knows only one barrier—love for the object." Also, p. 103 and p. 123 of the same reference.)

Re-emergence of the Dichotomy—1933

In 1933 we find further clarification of Freud's evolving views on this question: "it is in the middle of [the anal sadistic] phase, ... that consideration for the object makes its first appearance as a *precursor of a later erotic cathexis*" (p. 99; italics added). (In the Norton Edition, p. 135, the statement is translated as follows: "A forerunner of a later relation of love towards the object.")

While speaking of identification in relation to femininity, he reveals the character of this precursor to the later erotic cathexis of the phallic phase.

> A woman's identification with her mother allows us to distinguish two strata: the pre-Oedipus one which rests on her affectionate attachment to her mother, ... and the later one from the Oedipus complex which seeks to get rid of her mother. ... Much of both of them is left over for the future and ... neither ... is adequately surmounted in the course of development. But the *phase of the affectionate pre-Oedipus attachment is the decisive one for a woman's future* [p. 134; italics added].

Thus Freud returns with emphasis to the concept of a pre-oedipal affectionate attachment. Whether to adhere to a dichotomy in Eros based, on the one hand, upon a sensual current, and on the other, upon an affectional current that is object-directed earlier than the sensual component, is debatable. We believe that early during the second half of the first year of life, the affectional current becomes object-directed, and it originates directly in the experience of dependence on the object.

We have a last comment from Freud (1940) on this matter in *An Outline of Psychoanalysis*: "A child's first erotic object is the mother's breast that nourishes it. . . .

This first object is later completed into the person of the child's mother, who not only nourishes it but also looks after it and thus arouses in it a number of other physical sensations. By her care of the child's body she becomes its first seducer.[8] In these two relations [nourishment, satisfaction of dependent needs; and sexuality] lies the root of a mother's importance, unique without parellel, established unalterably for a whole lifetime as the first and strongest love-object and as the prototype of all later love relations—*for both sexes*" (p. 188; italics added).

Thus from 1933 on, we see the re-emergence of early statements on the relations of the two currents of libido—the affectional and the sensual—with the affectional current object-directed genetically the earlier of the two.

Comment

Through the length of Freud's writings, it appears that libido which is object directed differentiates into two component currents, the affectional and the sensual. In mature, genital object-relations, object cathexes consist of a mixture of affectional and sensual libido. Even when he broadened the concept of Eros to include all aspects of love with sensuality (1921, p. 90), affectional and sensual currents are clearly discernible conceptually as component currents of libido.

---

[8] A possible extension of this seduction thesis can be stated in terms of the seduction to dependence and affectional object love. In those terms, the mother's ministrations, physical and emotional, seduce the child into a dependent relationship which leads to object cathexis. Freud's historical point on the arousal of erotogenic zones by the mother's ministrations is applicable also to the development of dependence on love from the object, a ubiquitous development highly desirable for the further development of the individual's psychic organization and for civilization.

In his writings of early 1911-1913 and late 1926 and 1939, the affectional current of the libido emerges in the context of the child-mother relation, of need gratification, i. e., of dependence on the object. Even during the period when the question of two currents of the libido is sub-merged (1920-1925), the importance of the dependence on the object to the emergence of the object libido is clearly upheld: "The libido attaches itself to the satisfaction of the great vital needs, and chooses as its first objects the people who have a share in that process" (1921, p. 103). Genetically, the affectional current precedes the emergence of object-directed sensual libido which appears with the phallic phase of psycho-sexual development.

Since Freud's formulations, there have been noteworthy observations by ethologists (Lorenz, Hess and others) which have supported the hypothesis that the libidiniza-tion of the object with anaclitic-affectional libido *leads* to the attachment of the sensual (phallic) libido to that same object. In this sense, the sensual object-libido is anaclitic, it leans on the affectional libido—and we suggest that, in important measure, a sound affectional cathexis sets the stage for a sound sensual cathexis. Poor or defective libidi-nization of the object with affectional libido leads not only to labile and poor object relations, but must lead, as well, to poor and labile sensual cathexes. The prototype of object relations will be scarred and future object relations unfavorably biased. These theoretical considerations sug-gest another point. We have said that the sensual current follows the path formed by the affectional current. Opti-mal libidinization of dependence on the object then sets the stage for the Oedipus complex which it induces.

Freud stated many times from 1926 on that the condi-tion of helplessness of the human child under the impetus of the pleasure principle forges the libidinization of the object within the context of dependence of the child on his parent(s). Epigenetically, that earliest libidinization lies at the foundation of the psychic organization, and, from the standpoint of libido, continues throughout life in the affectional current of the libido.

PART II

THEORETICAL
CONSIDERATIONS

2. On the Genesis of Psychologic Dependence

INTRODUCTION

In this chapter we consider the nature of the emergence of psychological dependence in man. It is generally accepted that, to begin with, any neonate above a certain phylogenetic level is dependent on the adult for survival, and that its biologic dependence is determined by its helplessness, i. e., by the degree of its maturity at birth. Less clearly defined are the parts played in early development by instinctive mechanisms and by learning. Among animals, the status of neonatal psychophysiologic differentiation varies considerably. The more immature the neonate, the more altricial,[1] the more immature the central nervous system, and the less the capacity to perceive, to respond to

[1] According to Webster's *New International Dictionary* (1965) altricial comes from the Latin *altrix* which means female nourisher, and is derived from the verb *alere* "to nourish." *Altricial* is defined as "having the young hatched in a very immature and helpless condition so as to require care for some time."

73

stimuli, to execute motor acts, the less the capacity, too, for learning; also, the less operative those potential instinctive structures that subserve the development of object relations. Where object-seeking behavior occurs within several days after birth, much is ascribed to the function of instinctive structures (Lorenz, 1935, 1937; Hess, 1959; Harlow, 1962; Harlow et al., 1959, 1960, 1966; Liddell, 1957; Scott, 1963; Schneirla and Rosenblatt, 1961; Rosenblatt et al., 1962). But where time must elapse following birth before behavior indicative of object relatedness emerges, the operation of instinctive structures cannot easily be separated out from those psychic constructs acquired by learning (Schneirla and Rosenblatt, 1961; Rosenblatt et al., 1962; Schur, 1960).

Our interest in the respective roles instinctive mechanisms and experience play in determining the early psychic development in the altricial young leads us to a review of recent ethological studies. Psychoanalysis has already found it useful to apply to man what ethologists have learned from observing animals. For example, Spitz (1965b), Jacobson (1964), and Schur (1960) agree that Innate Releasing Mechanisms (IRMs) (Lorenz, 1935, 1937) play a significant part in human development. Then too, there has been the clarification stemming from the discussion of Bowlby's theory of the nature of the child's tie to its mother (A. Freud, 1960; Spitz, 1960; Schur, 1960; Jacobson, 1964), an issue directly relevant to the role played by dependence in the development of object relations in the human child. In the first (1958) of a series of thought-provoking papers, Bowlby hypothesized that the nature of this tie is determined by instinctive behavioral responses that lead to attachment of the child to the mother. Using an instinct model (energized by hydrodynamic principles) that does not take into account the interdigitating influence not only of instinctual drives, but also of the environment, Bowlby attempted to delineate the dynamics of the objectal tie.

We hope to show that there is considerable evidence to support Schur's (1960) suggestion, earlier stated by Freud with regard to neurosis and development (1937a; see Spitz, 1965b) and by Lorenz (1937, p. 151; 1935), that a complemental series of "innate versus acquired" factors best explains phylogenetic concepts of the development of the child and of his object relations. Schur observed that the higher one climbs the ladder of phylogeny, the greater the capacity for and the role of learning ("acquired") in adaptation to life, and that in man, the factor of instinctive ("innate") response patterns is greatly diluted and shadowed by learning.

PSYCHOANALYTIC OBSERVATIONS AND FORMULATIONS

In tracing psychoanalytic concepts of the nature of human development during the first year of life with respect to attachment to the object, we rely predominantly on the work of Spitz.

Piaget (1962) and Jacobson (1964) agree with Spitz (1960), who, quoting Malrieux, stated that

> Neither emotions and affects nor perceptions are available or differentiated at birth; they are developed interdependently, step by step. And a certain level of perceptual as well as emotional maturation and differentiation is the prerequisite for the maintenance of object relations .... Without the intervention of psychological processes, no object relations would ever be formed. We might have reflex behavior, but not interrelations of a reciprocal nature which ultimately lead to social relations. To experience these affects [grief and psychological pain], the infant has to develop a psychological organization [p. 87] ....

Although he here proposes that this development takes place around the sixth month of life, Spitz (1965b) later dates the beginnings of this psychological organization at about 6 weeks and suggests the emergence of the ego to be at about three months. He states that, prior to the sixth month, we have an "objectless stage" which extends from birth to three months and is followed by the "stage of the precursor of the object" extending from three to six months. This is followed by the emergence of the "libidinal object."

Mahler (1952 on) views the relation of the child to the mother from within a slightly different frame of reference. She notes that in the normal autistic phase the infant is indeed psychically objectless due to its nondifferentiation, i. e., neither ego nor instinctual drives are sufficiently differentiated. But the period from about two to three months onward is characterized by the development of a significant, albeit archaic, libidinal child-object relation, the normal symbiosis. Jacobson's (1964) formulations on this point corroborate those of Mahler. Spitz's six-month timetable for sufficient development of "a psychological organization" coincides with Mahler's formulations of the onset of the phase of separation-individuation which leads the child out of the normal symbiosis to the beginnings of object relations, as we know them in man. General agreement exists among child psychoanalysts (Spitz, Mahler, Jacobson, and others) that the libidinal object emerges at this period. Because the development of libidinal object relations is germane to our postulate of the libidinization of dependence, we will look at the observations of these investigators in some detail.

First Three Months of Life

State of differentiation at Birth. Spitz (1965b) has described the "objectless stage" as

> one of *non*differentiation, because the newborn's perception, activity, functioning are insufficiently organized into units except to a certain extent in areas which are indispensible for survival, like metabolism and nutritional intake, circulation, respiratory function and such. [In a footnote, he explains] My concept of nondifferentiation includes Hartmann's postulates [i. e., lack of differentiation between ego and id, conscious and unconscious of the newborn's personality]; . . . it takes in also . . . observable aspects, such as neuromuscular, physiological, behavioral aspects, for example, perception and action. In the stage of nondifferentiation, there is no clear distinction between psyche and soma, between inside and outside, between drive and object, between 'I' and 'Non-I,' and not even between different regions of the body [p. 35].

Jacobson (1964), we may add, suggests that the instinctual drives also are undifferentiated. This stage is perhaps one step further toward nondifferentiation than that suggested by Hoffer wherein "the object is drawn wholly into the internal narcissistic milieu and treated as part of it to the extent that self and object merge into one" (A. Freud, 1960, p. 56). This latter statement describes succinctly, we believe, the condition characteristic of early symbiosis. Hoffer's statement proposes later differentiation, more awareness, and infers action beyond that observable in human infants under six weeks of age.

We may push Spitz's comment farther than he intends by suggesting along with Jacobson (1954, 1964) that the degree of nondifferentiation of the human at birth creates difficulty with the concept of primary narcissism in the newborn. Jacobson (1964) finds primary narcissism a useful term but cautions, and we concur, that it "bears no reference to energic and structural differentiation and the corresponding establishment and cathexis of self and object representations" (pp. 15-16). We, too, find it useful for example, to explain the energics (albeit with insufficiently differentiated psychic energy) that cathect, however transiently, coenesthetic[2] experience. We believe that primary narcissism undergoes significant differentiation paralleling structural differentiation, particularly of primary autonomous ego functions. Such differentiation of primary narcissism is proposed by Mahler (1967) who points out that "*absolute* primary narcissism" changes to one wherein "not such absolute primary narcissism" prevails (p. 743). The altriciality of the human neonate represents a state of nondifferentiation of the psychic organization such that its psychophysiological beginnings must be reflexive (instinctive in the sense proposed by Lorenz [1935, 1953]), coenesthetic (Freud, 1940; Spitz, 1945b, 1965b; Schur, 1966; see also Mahler, 1952), mediated by primary autonomous functions of the ego (Hartmann, 1939, 1952) and operate on the nirvana principle, i. e., the organism seeks to maintain a constant level of minimal excitation. We believe (even if we have questions on the issue of primary narcissism in the newborn) that there is no evidence for "primary object-love" as suggested by the Balints (1953), and no evidence for primary object libido in the human newborn as suggested by Fairbairn (1954) and Guntrip (1961).

[2]i.e., an organization in which "sensing is extensive, primarily visceral, centered in the autonomic nervous system, and manifests itself in the form of emotions, an all-or-none phenomenon" (Spitz, 1965b p. 44).

Somato-Psychic Continuity: Reflexes, IRMs and the Environment. Spitz believes in the continuity from somatic to psychologic and observes that the prototypes for "psychic ego nuclei" are to be found in physiology and somatic behavior (1965b). In discussing the neurophysiological factors which underlie behavior in the newborn, he notes that "the infant shows quite a number of manifestations that have the semblance of responses and actions, some of them quite structured and complicated. They appear to be innate responses" (p. 43). In addition to reflex activity, such as respiration, temperature regulation and sucking reflexes, are the more complex rooting and smiling responses. The grasp and Moro(-like) reflexes are of interest too for our present concern. We draw attention to Harlow's (1966) suggestion that these latter reflexes belong, in the monkey, to an instinctive contact-clinging system. The human Moro reflex seems to have little actual function today except as an index of central nervous system maturation. We wonder, however, if it might not represent a manifestation or a residual of an innate attachment response of the type proposed by Harlow in monkeys. In a review article on the Moro reflex, Parmelee (1964) notes that it was considered by Moro himself to be a clinging type of reflex. We must quickly add that neither Parmelee nor many other pediatricians who followed Moro agreed with this concept. The grasp reflex, on the other hand, is possibly a more useful one for man. Spitz (1965b) observes that the grasp reflex, along with the rooting response, is among the most reliable of the reflexes. It may well activate prehension and, therefore, be important for hand and mouth integration (Hoffer, 1949)—in attaching the "thing" of exploration to oneself. Its use, however, for object contact-clinging in man is doubtful.

Innate response mechanisms (IRMs) are assumed to be part of the constitutional psycho-physiological givens of the human neonate not only by Spitz (1965b), but by Schur (1960) and Jacobson (1964) as well. Some neonatal reflexive patterns which guarantee self-preservation and the preservation of the species in monkeys by insuring attachment to the object most likely also occur as anlagen in man. Because in man, clinging is minimal if not altogether absent during the first five to six months of life, we believe that in man, the Moro and grasp reflexes largely represent phylogenetic residuals rather than mechanisms activated for object relations during the first few weeks of development. With the advent of the second half of the symbiotic phase, clinging mushrooms, not as a reflex, but as a dynamic response, principally in reaction to separation anxiety. Since the response appears under the threat of loss of the object, in man, the psychic existence of the object leads to the emergence of clinging behavior. This is the reverse of Bowlby's (1958) suggestion that in man, clinging, as a component instinct, *leads* to attachment. If indeed an IRM activates this clinging behavior in man, as it may, that IRM is activated by experience: fear of loss of the object. It is most probable that IRM's pertaining to sucking, crying, and smiling (Bowlby, 1958) do operate in early infant behavior and play an important part in the formation of the earliest object relation. But they do so, as Schur (1960) suggests, in interdigitation with the complex and vastly important influence of experience and learning.

Object Perception. According to Spitz (1950), during the first three months "environmental perception takes place only in function of the presence of a need-configuration directed towards this perception. The object, which at this period is to be considered a part object, is perceived only in function of the internal need. Therefore this period has to be considered objectless" (p. 140). Need-perception soon stimulates a gestalt of gratification which includes the gratifier as part of the self and of that gratification gestalt. The cognitive and affective experience of need-gratification is rooted in the physiologic experience of need-gratification. A. Freud (1947) observes:

> When it [the infant] is under the pressure of urgent bodily needs, as for instance hunger, it periodically establishes connections with the environment which are withdrawn again after the needs have been satisfied and the tension is relieved. These occasions are the child's first introduction to experiences of wish-fulfilment and pleasure. They establish centres of interest to which libidinal energy becomes attached. An infant who feeds successfully [eventually] 'loves' the experience of feeding (Narcissistic love) [p. 124].

In 1954 she states: "The libidinal cathexis at this time is shown to be attached, not to the image of the object, but to the blissful experience of satisfaction" (p. 12).

On the status of the neonate's cognitive capabilities, Spitz (1965b) comments that

> the newborn has no world image at all, no stimuli from any sensory modality that he can recognize as signals; even by the time he is six months old, only very few such signals have been established and laid down as memory traces. . . . Any stimulus will first have to be transformed into meaningful experience (p. 41). By far the most important factor in enabling the child to build gradually a coherent ideational image of his world derives from the reciprocity between mother and child. It is that part of object relations which I have called the "dialogue." The dialogue is the sequential action-reaction-action cycle within the framework of mother-child relations" (1965b, pp. 42-43).

Jacobson and Mahler have made the same point many times—that is, then by learning, and in accord with

Schneirla's hypothesis (see below). It seems to us that Spitz shys away from the model proposed by Hartmann of primary autonomous ego functioning, yet we need that principle to explain Spitz's observation that "memory traces [of experience] are laid down while [diacritic[3]] perception is being acquired" (1965b, p. 43).

Spitz (1965b) suggests that the beginnings of perception arise from contactual organs, the oral cavity (which has external and interoceptive receptors), the hand, labyrinth, and the skin. He observes, "To the neonate, the simultaneous sensations in the four sensory organs . . . are a proprioceptive total experience" (p. 74). And he notes of the shift from contact perception to distance perception by way of the visual apparatus: "I stressed the role of frustration . . . and how distance perception of the mother's face becomes differentiated from the unified experience of contact perception during nursing. . . . The nursing situation is not merely an experience of gratification. It initiates the transition from exclusive contact perception to distance perception. It activates the diacritic perceptual system" (p. 75).

Speaking ontogenetically then, Spitz states, "It is around the end of the first week of life that the infant begins to respond to cues. The first traces of aim-directed behavior appear, that is, activity, presumably associated with psychic process, which seems to take place according to the mode of the conditioned reflex" (p. 46). And he describes how, at about eight days of age, a breast-fed infant will turn its head toward the chest of the holder when raised in the horizontal feeding position. Between the ages of two to six weeks, he notes, in order to perceive

[3]The "diacritic organization" contrasts with the coenesthetic in that "perception takes place through peripheral sense organs and is localized, circumscribed, and intensive; its centers are in the cortex, its manifestations are cognitive processes, among them the conscious thought processes" (Spitz, 1965b, p. 44).

the external stimulus of the nipple, ". . . two factors must be present *jointly* and combine. The first is an external stimulus, the stimulus which the infant has come to associate with impending need gratification [the breast, or bottle, or mother] ; the second stimulus is of proprioceptive origin, . . . his need for food" (p. 48). Toward the beginning of the second month, the infant begins to perceive the object with some psychic meaning. At this time the crying baby will quiet at the approach of the adult. "In the course of the first six weeks of life a mnemonic trace of the human face is laid down in the infantile memory as the first signal of the presence of the need-gratifier" (p. 52). Now the adult face is a unique visual percept, preferred by the child over "things" in the environment (p. 86).

Second Three Months of Life

Spitz (1950) describes the second quarter of the first year of life as a transitional period, the stage of the precursor of the object. The precursors of the object are "characterized by the capacity to fulfill the exact requisite of a given need-configuration, [i.e.,] . . . they have a function" (p. 141). This suggests the slow emergence of awareness of the "need-satisfying function"[4] of the object and signals the introduction of the normal symbiotic phase of development. Mahler's (1952) observations referring to the first developmental hurdle are pertinent: the normal autistic phase gives way to the symbiotic one when the infant perceives that help comes from outside. Benedek (1956) suggests that the good experience becomes associated with

[4]Spitz, 1965b, Jacobson, 1964, and Schur, 1960, clearly indicate that need-satisfaction includes feeding, body care and contact, rocking, etc., i.e., physiologic, psychologic, and specifically libidinal, and not just oral satisfactions.

the good mother and the bad experience with the bad mother; eventually the affective quality of the internalized image of the mother is determined by the affective quality of these first experiences. According to A. Freud (1947, 1954) and Spitz (1965b), the need-gratification gestalt gradually becomes libidinized, and the mother is subsequently cognitively and libidinally differentiated out of these libidinized gestalts.

The stage of the precursor of the object extending from about the third to the sixth month, is heralded by that critical phenomenon, the "undifferentiated smiling response." If a human face, or its facsimile a mask, is presented frontally to the average three-month-old, he will smile rather indiscriminately. The profile of that same face will not elicit the same response. Spitz (1965b) notes (as does Mahler [1963, 1965]) that *it is "through the mother's instrumentality" that the infant has made a meaningful gestalt, the human face, out of a mass of meaningless environmental "things"* (p. 96). And he points out that "the process of selecting a meaningful entity from the universe of meaningless things and establishing it as a sign Gestalt is in the nature of a *learning* process" (p. 96; italics added).

Third Three Months of Life

In 1950 Spitz observed that

> in the third quarter ... true objects appear for the first time. They now have a face, but they still retain their function of a constituent part of the child's recently-established Ego. The loss of the object is therefore a diminution of the ego ... and is as severe a loss [as] of a large part of the body [symbiosis]. Anxiety is the effect evoked by the threatening imminence of such a loss [p. 141].

The object now acquires specificity for the child; its presence insures gratification of needs and its absence represents the first danger situation and leads to separation anxiety. This is the libidinal object. Spitz (1950) continues

> [T]he face which was the first visual sign by which the child recognized a partner as such remains also the leading perception in the further establishment of the libidinal object. This remains true even for the grown-up" (p. 141).[5]
>
> It is not accidental that at the anxiety signal's first inception [during the third quarter of the first year of life] we find the threat of a breakdown to the ego through the loss of its constituent part, the mother [p. 141].

That is, the mother is the object upon which the child is not only physically dependent, but is the object to whom it now becomes libidinally attached and upon whom it is dependent for gratification of emerging psychological (libidinal and nonlibidinal) needs. Spitz notes that the "object . . . is already libidinal object on one hand, but still a constituent part of the Ego on the other. It is at this turning-point of the development that the basic security and the basic insecurity of the child and later on of the adult is laid down. Here is the beginning of so many severe neurotic and psychotic conditions" (p. 141). It is here, just past the peak of the normal symbiotic phase of development, that the process of separation-individuation begins (Mahler, 1965, 1968b). Indeed, it is here that the child begins to exhibit behaviorally a psychologic dependence on his mother and here that psychologic dependence emerges in its maximum of intensity.

[5]This, in certain respects, bears a resemblance to imprinting in terms of the attraction valence of the percept of the object and in the attachment to that percept. What both phenomena achieve, whether by imprinting, or by a complemental process of IRMs and learning is the attachment to an object of the species. See below.

Recapitulation: Differentiation of the Libidinal Object

We recapitulate briefly Spitz's view of the earliest differentiation of the libidinal object as it emerges in man. We
assume that the reason the infant at birth shows no indication—cognitive or affective—of object perception is that
there is insufficient differentiation of psychic function for
such perception.

From about six weeks to three months on, a most dramatic phenomenon appears: the undifferentiated smiling
response (Spitz, 1946a, 1965). This response results from a
learning process: the "selection of a meaningful entity—the
face-gestalt—from a universe of meaningless things" (Spitz,
1965b, p. 96).

From the stage of the undifferentiated smile, the infant
moves to that of the differentiated smile aroused by the
emerging libidinal object (Spitz, 1965b). The infant gradually discriminates more and more between the specific object (mother) and objects other-than-mother. (Father and
siblings stand in a more or less intermediate position between the valence ascribed to the mother and strangers.)
The infant passes through a series of perceptual and affective responses to the presentation of faces other-than-
mother (excepting father and siblings)—that is, the spec-
trum of "stranger responses." With the synthesis of the
libidinal object, separation anxiety and stranger responses
make their appearance frequently.

In closing, we quote Schur (1960):

> The human infant is an altricial creature *par excellence.* It is
> utterly dependent . . . on external help for any satisfaction of its
> needs which cannot be satisfied by automatic, homeostatic regula-
> tions. . . . It learns to connect a 'mother' figure with the source of
> all these 'physiological' and psychological 'nutriments.' It enters

the 'symbiotic' phase . . . where self-awareness and body image start to develop—where, however, self and objects are not really differentiated. . . . With locomotion and increasing regard for the environment the infant becomes aware of all kinds of . . . dangers . . . . The child develops also the *recognition of his own helplessness* [italics added]. . . . This helplessness is the expression of the weakness of his own rudimentary ego which can be overcome only through his 'external executive' ego . . . the mother (p.77).

NOTES FROM ANIMAL OBSERVATIONS

Imprinting

Let us now turn, for purposes of clarification, to consider some recent studies of neonate behavior in species other than man.[6]

There have been significant observations in ethology since 1958, when Bowlby applied findings from this field to psychoanalytic theory of child development. In a summarizing and updating article, Hess (1959) states that "early social contacts determine the character of adult social behavior" (p. 133). This is satisfactory to any student of child development, whatever his frame of reference. He notes that imprinting to date is understood to be an instinctive attachment response which occurs in some precocial[7] neonates in reaction to perceptual pattern of an object, animate or inanimate. He observes that Lorenz (1935, 1953) defined the principle of imprinting, which had been reported by others but not so identified, as a "particular kind of conditioning" that is "limited to a very definite

[6]Obviously our review of the relevant literature has not been an exhaustive one. Lack of time and energy rob us of such luxury. We especially regret excluding from this study the animal work done by I. C. Kaufman, P. Seitz, and J. Masserman.

[7]Species whose young are born in a state of CNS maturation that allows for a significant degree of cognitive, affective, and motor functioning.

and often extremely short phase of ontogeny ... is ... quite irreversible ... [and] takes place quite independently of whether the activity released by the stimulus is ... functional or not" (p. 115). Lorenz (1935, 1953) observed that imprinting in greylag geese appeared during a critical period[8] early in the animal's life. Imprinting has been studied mainly in birds, but it has also been reported in insects and fish, as well as in sheep, deer, and buffalo (Hess, 1959)[9].

Hess (1959) demonstrated, in mallard ducks and certain other birds, that some imprinting occurs immediately after hatching, that it occurs maximally in ducklings 13 to 16 hours of age and that the critical period for imprinting passes in these ducks at about 24 hours of age. He observed that the emergence of fear of a strange or novel object coincides with and indicates the end of that critical period. The fear of the object leads to the response of withdrawal, escape from the object, which is antagonistic to the response of imprinting—approaching and following the object. "The rapid drop of imprinting, then, appears to be coupled with the developing of the emotional response of fear" (p. 159). One might ask whether this onset of the fear response in the duckling may have a corollary in the anxiety reaction to the stranger observed from about four to six months on in the human infant. Indeed, Hess suggested that if imprinting is to be found in the human infant, its critical period would terminate with the onset of manifest fear, at about five-and-a-half months. (Hess's interesting suggestion is taken up by P. H. Gray [1958]—see below.)

[8]In general, critical period hypothesis holds that if a given ontogenetic differentiation does not occur during a specific phase of maturation that particular differentiation will not occur at any time.

[9]Lorenz (1935, 1953) has made it clear, as has Hess (1959), that not all precocial young exhibit imprinting to nonspecies objects.

In their field tests of imprinting, Hess demonstrated that decoy-imprinted ducklings attached to these inanimate mechanized decoys, whereas unimprinted mallards about a day old (that is, past the critical period for imprinting), attached rapidly to live female mallards but not to the decoys. He herewith demonstrated that laboratory imprinting a duckling to an inanimate decoy can interfere with the "natural" instinctive response of following, or attaching to the natural mother. Therefore, we might say that, in this case, laboratory imprinting, itself the experimental product of an instinctive response, interfered with the emergence of the natural instinctive response to the actual maternal object. We can assume that such an artifactual imprinting can occur in nature as well (although Lorenz [1953] believes it happens little, if at all). The strength of this species-preservative phenomenon—which led to decoy imprinting—is evidence of the receptive status and the degree of differentiation of the brain of these precocial neonates.

Hess also observes that ducks released at one day of age will ignore the decoy object, but will go to the live female ducks immediately, even though they had been exposed to neither decoy nor live female before (1959). Thus, as he suggested, socialization is not solely determined by imprinting in these organisms.

These observations support the hypothesis that imprinting is a powerful instinctive mechanism which, in the first day of life of these ducks, secures attachment to the object. Lorenz has proposed (1935, 1953) that where imprinting occurs it is the product of an innate releasing mechanism (IRM) which is not influenced by learning. The stimulus that may activate this mechanism requires certain characteristics (i. e., in size, shape, color, motility, etc.), but it seems to be independent of the inherent character or function of that external stimulus. For our present concern, we underscore the criterion that imprinting is not a learned behavior, but rather totally innate behavior activated *prior to any valuation of the object or of the experience* in the context of which this behavior occurs.

Let us here point out three postulates of early object attachment suggested by imprinting: (1) object attachment is not restrained by species boundaries. (This supports the concept of a powerful need for object attachment.) (2) the earliest attachment, here specifically, imprinting, has a long-range effect and is irreversible. (3) sexual behavior is channelled to the object of earliest attachment. In terms of postulates (1) and (2), interspecies attachment is well-known; the relationship between domesticated dog, horse and other pets[10] with man can, at times, be awesome. In terms of postulate (3), mounting behavior of a dog upon the leg of a house guest, to the embarrassment of the host, derives from such early attachment to humans, an extra-species object to which sexual impulses are directed. Lorenz "postulated that the first object to elicit a social response ... later released not only that response but also related responses such as sexual behavior" (Hess, 1959, p. 133). In addition to other such reports, Hess also notes a case of a jungle-fowl cock which was imprinted by him and kept away from its species for the first month: "This animal even after five years—much of that time in association with his own species—courts human beings with typical behavior, but not females of his own species" (1959 p. 140). If we assume that imprinting is a *special case*[11] of the attachment of the young to a parental object, we can extend these postulates to human behavior as well, what-

[10]If imprinting occurs in the dog and cat, it varies in significant characteristics from the imprinting described by Lorenz and Hess.

[11]Lorenz identifies imprinting as "a particular kind of conditioning that ... differs from other types of learning" (1953, p. 115). This remains to be clarified.

ever the nature of the mechanisms for earliest attachment to the object. Postulate (3) is relevant to Freud's observations (1905 on) that the sexual, genital impulses are experienced first in relation to the object of earliest attachment, the mother. Freud's (1920) theory of Eros, on which the broader theories of libido and object relations are based, is graphically represented in these instinctive mechanisms and behaviors.

In the species that imprint object attachment seems rapidly secured in the neonate. Interference with such attachment instinctive structures, can have long-lasting consequences. We see in the demonstration by Liddell (1958) the remarkably disruptive influence—disruptive of instinctive mother-child patterns—of separating a mother goat from her newborn kid. Five minutes after birth he separated a twin kid from its mother and sibling for only one hour. He observed significant differences between the twins in patterns of attachment to the mother, to the flock, as well as in their personalities and physical development thereafter.

Imprinting as described by Lorenz and Hess is manifested by the neonate staying in close proximity to and following the imprinted object. Scott, however reports that imprinting of chicks has been effected without following, "although muscular tension may still be important" (1962, p. 951). This may suggest that imprinting does not relate principally to motor activity, although Scott agrees with Hess that the degree of emotional arousal, or energy expended by the neonates, accelerates and intensifies the imprinting response. The point we wish to underscore here is: what determines the capacity of the neonate to execute instinctive structures, i. e., to attach, is the degree of maturity of its central nervous system manifested, in this instance, in the degree of executive (motor) capability. It is our impression, furthermore, that both Scott and Hess suggest affective responsiveness in the precocial organism which would parallel the noteworthy degree of maturation of its motor and cognitive apparatuses. In contrast, the maturation of the altricial organism's central nervous system lags significantly beyond its fetal state. It would seem that imprinting as described by Lorenz and Hess is a phenomenon requiring sufficient maturation of the central nervous system to allow for a sufficient capability of cognitive and executive—and perhaps affective as well—functioning, functioning not yet achieved in the altricial young. We may therefore assume that a different system of securing the establishment of attachment to the object occurs in the altricial organism.

From observing exactly such an organism, the domesticated cat, Schneirla (1961) and his coworkers (Rosenblatt, et al., 1962) have hypothesized the interrelation of maturation of innate givens and experience in object attachment and development. They observe that in the cat, "suckling occurs within the first hour after birth. . . . In this period . . . feedings are initiated mainly by the female. *She* approaches the kittens . . ." (pp. 199-200, italics added). They find that, in the development of socialization in the kitten, step by step differentiations result from the interactions of kitten and mother. And Schneirla has emphasized "the basic role of recriprocal stimulative processes in mammalian social ontogeny, in relation to factors of maturation and of experience postulated as inextricably interrelated in individual development" (Rosenblatt, et al., 1962, p. 199; also Schneirla, Rosenblatt, 1961, p. 231).

Primary Socialization

Another such altricial animal studied is the domesticated dog. J. P. Scott (1963) addresses himself to this issue.

He postulates that "primary socialization . . . is the way in which the young animal of any species becomes attached to other members of the same species" (p. 2). He generalizes from the observations on imprinting, suggesting that "Imprinting is the avian counterpart of a phenomenon widespread in the animal kingdom, namely the existence of a short period early in development when primary social relationships are established" (p. 3). Scott eventually makes it clear that by "primary" he does mean "instinctive," and he suggests that primary socialization means a process directed by "instinctive social reactions." He observes, however, that the process of forming the first relationship involves "both the primary or instinctive social reactions of the species and the capacity for learning" (p. 4).

Scott (1963) presents a vital hypothesis of *primary socialization*. However, he clouds the hypothesis that *reciprocity and complementation in maturation (innate givens) and experience (acquired factors) are operative* in very early social ontogeny, particularly in the altricial young. He sees imprinting not as a "complete process" in the formation of object relations, but rather as "only the beginning of a process" (p. 6). In one sense, this is correct; in another, it is unsatisfactory. We believe it is correct in that socialization in precocial organisms that imprint goes beyond the process and period for imprinting; Hess (1959) suggested this too. In this sense, *imprinting is a special case of primary socialization.* Much occurs beyond imprinting between the subject and object to attain socialization typical for the species. However, imprinting as described by Lorenz and Hess is indeed "complete" in the sense that it is binding, indelible, and an irrevocable mechanism. It occurs near birth and is independent of experience; it is not anaclitic (based on experience) in the psychoanalytic sense. Certainly it requires a stimulus from the environment, but the stimulus has no experience value, according to Lorenz (1953). Metapsychologically, it is a process that structures a mental representation in the psychic organization, that binds a powerful libidinal cathexis, already differentiated, soon after birth, and therewith determines the fate of later differentiating genital cathexes.

To return to Scott's observations: he points out that primary socialization in puppies does not occur until they are *three weeks of age.* By this time the puppy attains partial independence from the mother and responds increasingly to litter mates. Scott notes that, after the neonatal period (first 14 days), comes the transitional period during which "the behavior of the puppy is transformed into the adult type. Within the space of a week the young pup is changed from a wormlike creature, which mostly feeds, rests, and eliminates, into a recognizable young dog. *It is only when this is done that the period and the process of socialization begins.* [!] The puppy then starts to form true social relationships with the mother, the litter mates", etc. (1963 pp. 5-6; italics added).

Scott's data, as well as Rosenblatt and Schneirla's observations, suggest an important complication in determining the character of the genesis of the first object relations in the altricial organism: the occurrence of a *neonatal period of insufficient somatopsychic differentiation,* during which the nature of relating to the object is overdetermined and obscure. On the basis of this insufficient differentiation, we believe that classical imprinting as described by Lorenz and Hess does not occur in altricial animals. Although Scott observes that with the puppies, as with Rosenblatt and Schneirla's kittens, it is the mother who initiates feeding and interaction, he disregards this fact and suggests that socialization in puppies begins only at three weeks of age.[12]

Scott's Observation on Human Infants. Scott (1963) attempts to study the development of socialization, of object relations, in canine and human infants. His effort is a synthesizing one. He compares indices of maturation such as feeding, locomotion, sensory capacity, nervous system myelinization, learning processes, and language; also, certain responses such as crying and smiling, as well as physiological responses such as heart rate and breathing associated with fear. He gives the impression that in his experiences, the developmental data of both organisms are quite comparable, with the exception of certain species-specific characteristics such as smiling and language development which the dog does not share with man.

Reviewing data on conditioning in human infants, Scott observes that conditioning in the newborn (under 10 days) is unstable and the "Conditioning of the sucking response to sound may be stable as early as 30 days and is probably present in most infants by 45 days (six weeks). Conditioning of the wink reflex to sight of movement is stable by 70 days, ... indicating the development of the capacity for visual perception" (p. 20). Scott notes then that according to present knowledge, certain maturational processes in the human allow for conditioning to occur by six to 10 weeks of age. This suggests that the infant will have suffi-

---

[12]In ducks, Hess observed "some imprinting occurs immediately after hatching" (1959, p. 135). Hess's table indicates 50 percent imprinting response at birth, with a maximal of such responses at 13 to 16 hours of age. In contrast to the pup and the kitten, a number of mammalian neonates, the calf, the foal, the young of goats, sheep and deer, and others, show socialization behavior within hours of birth.

cient capacity for cognition so that he can ascribe certain characteristics to an external event resulting from the acquired knowledge that this event will cause pain or gratification. Thus, by six weeks, he may perceive that crying leads to the gratification-gestalt.

Referring to Spitz (1946a) and Ambrose (1960), Scott (1963) observes that the smiling response appears at about six weeks of age and believes it has no other function than its social one. Pointing to the time of the emergence of the smiling response he notes that Spitz and Wolf (1946a) reported very few orphanage babies to have smiled at the sight of a face at two months, whereas up to nearly 100 per cent of infants of three-to-five-months did so. "By six months of age the percentage of babies smiling at faces of strangers had dropped almost to zero, although they continued to smile at the faces of familiar persons" (p. 23). This, Scott believes, indicates that the process of primary socialization had taken place. The emergence of fear of the stranger, described in conjunction with the smiling response, supports one aspect of Scott's effort to correlate primary socialization with imprinting: i.e., the anxiety produced by the stranger in the six-month-old infant would satisfy the criterion for termination of the critical period for imprinting (if such occurs in humans). Gray (1958), also in great measure stretching the concept of imprinting, suggests that the smiling response is "the motor equivalent of the following response in animals below the higher primates" (p. 160).

Scott concludes that all of the data indicate that in the human infant, *the period between five or six weeks and five or six months of age is the period of primary socialization* (p. 25). Scott observes that Gray (1958) proposed this period as that for imprinting in the human infant.

"Primary socialization," perhaps; "imprinting," no. Although this time period may satisfy some of the criteria for imprinting, particularly its termination with the appearance of stranger anxiety, important differences exist between the primary socialization of altricial organisms and that of organisms which imprint.

What happens during the blanked-out five to six weeks following birth? According to Scott, simple conditioning[13] may occur by six weeks. Indeed Spitz, as we have already mentioned, reports conditioning at a much earlier age. Fragmentary cognitive processes must begin to take place earlier. The six-week-old human infant is manifestly very different from the totally blind-to-awareness neonate. Can he be conditioned by six weeks to the pattern: hunger—cry—nondifferentiated "object-I" appears with breast or bottle—satisfaction of need? This pattern might have occurred on the average about 200 times in six weeks. Moreover we have reduced the mother-child interaction to its bare minimum of feeding interaction only. We are not even considering the emotional arousal and libidinal "feeding" along with the many additional stimuli, the talking to, touching, cuddling, wiping and washing, the visual stimuli, etc., which intensify and enrich contact, well before any manifestation of attachment or "object" perception occurs on the part of the human child.

We conclude that not enough is made by Scott (1963) or Gray (1958) of the period *preceding* that of primary socialization. We concur with Schneirla et al. (1961, 1962), who point to the complex interdigitations and reciprocal influencing of maturational factors and environmental experience during that neonatal period. We suggest

[13.]The conditioning to which we here refer is not imprinting.

—in terms of evolutionary process—that in the altricial young, *this period of neonatal insufficient differentiation has made certain instinctive attachment mechanisms inoperative and has increased the influence of the caretaking environment on the development of the first object relations.* We propose that during the neonatal period of insufficient differentiation in the human infant (i. e., the period prior to six or so weeks of age), imprinting, as described by Lorenz and Hess, cannot occur.

Object Relations in Primates

We turn now to the work of Harlow, work of particular interest to our hypothesis. Harlow's studies are of noteworthy relevance to psychoanalytic theory of child development and of object relations, when viewed in the light of Mahler's formulations on normal symbiosis and separation-individuation in the human child.

Of primates, i. e., monkeys, apes and man, Harlow (1960) proposes five affectional systems: infant for mother; peer for peer; the heterosexual affectional pattern; the maternal and perhaps a paternal affectional pattern. He suggests that

> in primates the primary tie of the infant for the mother is achieved through the operation of two dominant systems; a system associated with the breast and the act of nursing and a system developed around contact, or to use Bowlby's term, 'contact-comfort.' Both mechanisms can be demonstrated to be operating during the infant monkey's *first day of life* as a group of reflexes [1960, p. 677; italics added].

In 1966, Harlow describes four stages of the infant-mother affectional system in monkeys, his principal subject having been the rhesus macaque: (1) the reflex stage;

(2) the stage of comfort and attachment; (3) the security stage; (4) the separation stage. For our present purposes, we shall describe only the first and second stages.

The *reflex stage* in the monkey lasts about 10 to 20 days, and is characterized by behavior considered to be of a physiologic and instinctive, reflex nature. "[The reflexes] include orienting the head up, hand and foot grasping, clasping, 'climbing' and rooting, sucking, righting, and contactual following" (p. 249). In 1960, Harlow commented on the nature of contacting and clinging reflexes. He observed that when a neonate monkey is placed in a supine position it will generally reflexly right itself into a prone position. "If, however, a baby monkey is placed on its back and then permitted contact with either a soft cylindrical object or a wire cylinder, it will clasp the object and make no effort to right itself. . . . Thus, it appears that contacting and clinging are special primitive postural reflexes" (p. 677). And he notes that the hand and foot grasp reflexes are also part of this contacting system. We add, in passing, that perhaps the Moro reflex in the human neonate as well as the powerful and longer-lasting grasp reflexes may represent neurophysiologic counterparts in the human infant.

In the rhesus neonate, these "reflex behaviors are supplanted after 10 to 20 days of age by partially, then totally, voluntary responses." This brief reflex period, Harlow notes, "serves to guarantee survival by assuring proper orientation to and contact with the mother's body, nourishment, and physical support when the infant is unable to control its own movements. Socialization begins during this period when the baby's tie to the mother is involuntary. . . . Primarily, however, it is a stage of physical adjustment rather than socialization" (1966, p. 249). Harlow's reports lead us to believe that only the first part of this period is *the neonatal period of insufficient differentia-*

tion; and that period (first 10 days) is brief in comparison with that of the human infant (approximately six to 16 weeks) and that of the dog (about three weeks).

During the *comfort and attachment stage*, the second stage, "true affectional bonds between offspring and mother are formed and basic social relationships are established." The infant monkey "maintains close physical contact with the mother through mechanisms associated with nursing, mechanisms associated with intimate body contact, and mechanisms which enable the infant to follow and to imitate appropriate maternal behaviors" (Harlow and Harlow, 1966, p. 249).

Comparative observations of the data on monkeys and man reveal a marked variance in biologic differentiation between the two. Harlow states (1960, 1966) that the monkey matures at a rate four times that, and the ape at twice that of the human infant. Moreover, the difference between monkey and human in the length of time it takes for comparable cognitive, affective, and motor functioning to appear, suggests that the monkey neonate's CNS is significantly more mature than the human's.[14]

Contact-Comfort in Primates. Harlow (1959) carried out a basic experiment to evaluate the various behaviors operative (according to Harlow, principally nursing and contact-comfort) in the development of affectional ties in monkeys. Eight monkey neonates between 6 to 12 hours of age were placed in individual cages, each with both a cloth and

[14]We have insufficient data on the monkey neonate to satisfactorily comment on the comparative state of the human and monkey *at birth* with reference to their respective degrees of altriciality. Relevant, however, is a note from Ribble (1943) who states that the rhesus assists his own birth by ". . . pulling himself out of the birth canal, after which he climbs to the breast and clings with arms around [the mother's] body or neck" (pp. 11-12). If that note is accurate, it places even more distance between the human's altriciality and the monkey's precocity than we have assumed here.

a wire mother-surrogate.[15] For four of the monkeys, only
the wire surrogate lactated by a protruding, milk-yielding,
rubber nipple; for the other four, only the cloth surrogate
lactated. Over the period of at least 165 days, the development of affectional responsiveness was evaluated in various
testing situations. Harlow's data (1959, p. 422), consisting
of contact time and nursing time per day during the first
25 days and the first 165 days, indicate that during the
first 25 days of age there was a notable S-shaped increment
in *contact time* with the cloth surrogate in those four infants who took their feeding from the wire surrogate. *The
maximal incrementation occurred between 15 to 20 days
of age.* Associated with this was a very shallow and insig-
nificant increase in *nursing time* in these same "wire-fed"
infants. The data suggest that from the first exposure (at
six or so hours of age) to the two surrogates, the cloth one
was used approximately six hours per day by those infants
whose wire surrogate lactated, and about nine hours per
day by those whose cloth surrogate lactated. Obviously the
latter could get both soft contact and milk from the same
surrogate. As might be expected, during the first 25 days
the "cloth-fed" monkeys had an earlier increment in time
spent in contact with their (lactating) cloth surrogate. In
these monkeys the increase in contact time followed a
fairly straight line. From 25 to 30 days on (during the
stage of "comfort and attachment"), the peak of contact
time per day was obtained (17 hours) for both "cloth-fed"
and "wire-fed" infants and decreased minimally over the
remainder of the 165-day period recorded. Harlow noted
that both groups showed a distinct preference for the cloth

[15] Although we use Harlow's term "mother-surrogate," we believe that
they are neither mothers nor surrogates in the psychoanalytic sense. That is,
they are not "objects"; they are inanimate cloth and wire "things." Harlow
himself is well-aware of this distinction (personal communication).

mother. He tells us, however, that these data do not obtain statistical significance (note that the number of subjects studied was small); still, they cannot be ignored. And one is impressed by the picture of an infant monkey holding on to his cloth surrogate with his feet for "contact-comfort" while stretching out so as to reach his nearby wire surrogate for nourishment (in the case where the wire surrogate was the lactating object) (1960, p. 680).

Bearing in mind Mahler's formulations with reference to normal symbiosis and separation-individuation, we quote Harlow (1959):

> These data make it obvious that contact-comfort is a variable of critical importance in the development of affectional responsiveness to the surrogate mother, and that nursing appears to play a negligible role. With increasing age and opportunity to learn, an infant fed from a lactating wire mother does not become more responsive to her as would be predicted from a drive-derived theory, but instead becomes increasingly more responsive to its non-lactating cloth mother [p. 423].

This extremely interesting finding suggests to us that attachment behavior very likely has instinctive roots and is represented neurophysiologically by highly-developed reflex attachment patterns which can be executed by an infant rhesus monkey because of its relative maturity at birth and the rate of maturation of its cognitive and motoric functions.

In fear-producing test situations, "the cloth mother was highly preferred to the wire mother (as a source of security), and ... these differences were unrelated to feeding conditions" (Harlow and Zimmerman, 1959, p. 423).[16] Harlow reported that, in such fear-producing situations, in

---

[16]In other studies, Harlow found that a lactating cloth mother was preferred to a cloth mother that did not lactate (personal communication).

the presence of the cloth surrogate, after some "rubbing their bodies about hers," the infant monkeys lose their fear and may approach the object of fright (p. 423). In contrast, the absence of the surrogate in such test situations leads to "either freezing in a crouched position . . . or running around the room on the hind feet, clutching themselves with their arms" (p. 426).

Clinging in Primates. Harlow's efforts to determine the importance of clinging (as distinct from contact-comfort) showed that up to 180 days of age, the infants preferred lying on a cloth plane to clinging to the cloth cylinder; from then on the preference shifted to the cylinder. Harlow suggested that the plane provided greater comfort than the cylinder; and he drops this possibly disappointing but interesting matter without, to the best of our knowledge, further discussion. We can only infer from Harlow's reports that clinging and contact-comfort are different components of attachment behavior. The above data could suggest that in these monkeys contact-comfort takes precedence over clinging. It may well be that clinging insures contact-comfort and has its importance in that function.

Yet have we disposed of the clinging reaction? After observating infant monkeys reared in pairs or multiples, but without a mother or surrogate (i. e., wire or cloth), Harlow reports a striking clinging reaction. In these neonates *during the "reflex stage"* (the first 10 to 20 days after birth), "if they succeed in contacting each other, they cling reflexly as they do to their mothers and follow each other between episodes of clinging and clasping. When two infants are together, the clinging typically assumes a ventral-ventral clasp" (1966, p. 254). The photographed ventral-ventral clasp like the usual human embrace is a most striking picture of clinging. We have seen phenomenologically similar infant-to-mother clinging in human infants in the latter part of the normal symbiotic phase of development—at six to 10 months. But this clinging occurs under conditions that produce anxiety and not on a reflex basis.

Harlow (1966) goes on . . .

> when more than two are together, the pattern tends to be a 'choo-choo' formation, —a chain of infants, one in the lead and one at the end and with intermediate infants clinging to the back of the infant in front of it. In keeping with [their] motor limitations at this stage of development, there is little activity other than clinging and following.[17] If the animals remain together in a cage without interference, the clinging is interrupted by only brief respites and then resumes. . . . This behavior tends to become fixated and to persist long after the clinging reflex disappears if the infants are kept together continuously from early infancy. This clinging fixation is comparable to that observed in infant monkeys raised with cloth surrogates. [Note the similar fixation of clinging to both other-than-mother surrogates: peer and inanimate object.] It cannot occur in live-mother-raised infants because the mother actively prevents continuous clinging. . . . Similarly, under natural conditions the infant would have no opportunity to display reflex clinging to another infant because mothers prevent their babies from venturing beyond arms' reach during this early period of life. [We note with interest this paradoxical behavior.] *[T]he nature of the behavior when restraint is lacking merely reflects the primary need and the limited behavioral repertoire of the neonatal monkey* [pp. 254-255, our italics].

We do not reject the proposition of primary need for clinging in monkeys; but we are puzzled by the assumption that continuous clinging (i. e., a release of instinctive clinging) in these rhesus infants results from lack of maternal restraint. We believe it is more complex than that—even in rhesus macaque.

[17]In contrast, the human infant, during the neonatal period, can neither cling, nor follow.

We remind our reader that present psychoanalytic theory of child development holds that the ego's capacity for awareness and recognition of specific objects in the external environment, and its experiencing of anxiety gradually reach functional level at about the age of five to six months in the human child.

Harlow has repeatedly stressed, and his observations seem to confirm, that the monkey neonate is *much more mature* than the human neonate. This seems to us to be borne out in the pictures of the first phase monkeys ventrally-clasped (1966, p. 253) and the "choo-choo"-clasped chain of infants (p. 254) who seem clearly in visual contact with the photographer and seem comparable to human infants five to eight months of age in terms of the affect their picture conveys, the quality of awareness of the environment they suggest, and the motoric capability reported. We see such affect and similar, but not reflexive, clinging in normal development of human children under conditions that threaten the presence of the mother, i. e., separation anxiety. This clinging makes its appearance, and may be intense and frequent, during the second half of the first year of life. It is part of the normal symbiotic phase of development.

We question that the excessive clinging in rhesus monkeys results from lack of restraint on the part of the absent mother and reflects the primary need to cling. We find from the data referred to above that the wire-fed, surrogate-raised neonates remained in contact with the cloth surrogate six hours at the outset and that the maximal increment of contact time occurred *between 15 to 20 days of age*, and reached its peak at 25 to 30 days of age, during the second phase of the infant-mother affectional system. It would seem that some event takes place that leads to the sigmoid increase in contact time in the wire-fed infants. Also of interest is the fact that the cloth-fed neonates' increment of clinging was more gradual and does not demonstrate the cloth attachment factor as clearly. To assume that the first-stage monkey is too immature motorically to attain the object is refuted by the data: it does reach the surrogate and can rest at its base. Once reached, it would seem that the cloth surrogate would be clung to with impunity. There seemed to be, instead, an *increasing* need to seek contact. We suggest that the factor responsible might be the gradual development of awareness of the external environment by the infantile monkey ego with consequent development of fear of the environment as a result of the helplessness of that infantile ego. We recall that the "reflex stage" in the monkeys in question lasts 10 to 20 days. We are impressed with the degree of maturation of the monkey in terms of cognitive, motoric and affective capabilities in the latter part of the "reflex phase." Then too, the maximal increment of contact time, an activity that requires by its characteristics a considerable degree of monkey ego-functioning, occurred between 15 to 20 days. The possibility for increasing degrees of anxiety (affect) correlating with increasing awareness (cognition) by the ego is compatible with the data. Could the infant monkey at 10 to 20 days of age still be responding only reflexly and yet show as marked a degree of awareness of the environment as seems manifested by the infant monkeys photographed by Harlow? We believe it is not presumptive to assume the appearance of anxiety late in the first-phase monkeys. We do not question the observations of the investigators that clinging behavior is reflexive in the neonate and perhaps in the 10-or-so-days-old monkey. But we do question Harlow's conclusion that it is the lack of maternal restraint that leads to fixation of a reflexive clinging response in the *10- to 20-days-old* motherless monkeys. We are not convinced that this observation helps to substantiate the hypothesis that clinging is a primary, instinctive need.

Evidence for Instinctive Attachment in Monkeys. More convincing evidence in Harlow's data for instinctive attachment in rhesus monkeys, we believe, obtains in the phenomenon of attachment to the cloth, inanimate "thing". That the "thing" becomes "object" is striking evidence, we believe, of instinctive contact-comfort-clinging behavior in these monkeys. This phenomenon has a strong resemblance to Winnicott's transitional object (1953): it is inanimate, has numerous functions (care, comfort, protection, etc.) and is the object of many impulses—affectionate, attachment, aggressive. There is an important distinction, however, between the two phenomena. The transitional object is cathected with libido that is withdrawn from the actual mother and displaced onto, indeed, the surrogate-mother. Not so in Harlow's monkeys. Harlow's surrogate-mothers are neither surrogates nor mothers, they are "things" that become "objects" by virtue of their having been ascribed a function—as of protection. We venture the suggestion that the level of differentiation of the monkey infant allows for a degree of differentiation of libido that makes a quantity of that libido readily accessible to instinctive attachment mechanisms. We are proposing, in other words, that the human infant's transitional object owes its existence to part of the libido previously attached to the mother being withdrawn from her and attached to the inanimate object which is experientially a substitute for her. In Harlow's monkeys, there were no actual mothers (we make no allowance for the six hours post parturition, perhaps unjustifiably); the cloth object was the *first* thing to become object. Inasmuch as all relation to that cloth object was nonreciprocal and unilateral, we assume that instinctive behavior on the infant's part may account for the attachment. Harlow seems not to have raised this point. This phenomenon, in particular, suggests the existence of instinctive attachment mechanisms in the monkey.

Harlow (1966) proposes a reflex phase of 10 to 20 days prior to the development of what he calls "true"[18] affectional bonds. Within the limitations of these data, we agree with Harlow that the immaturity of the human neonate is much greater than that of the monkey neonate which, by perhaps less than 10 days of age, shows an awareness of the environment, affective responsiveness and motoric development suggestive of five to eight months of age in the human. Thus we might suggest a "neonatal period of insufficient differentiation" of less than ten days in the monkey. We believe that this factor is of great consequence to the evolution of the complemental series of "innate vs. acquired" attachment determinants in rhesus monkeys.

One further note on Harlow's observations with regard to the nature of contact-comfort in monkey object-relations. Harlow's monkeys showed the need for proximity with the object, i. e., for being attached to the object. This behavior is suggestive of the psychoanalytic concepts of normal symbiosis (Mahler, 1952 on) and separation anxiety in development, wherein the infant is in a libidinal and apperceptual state of oneness with the mother. Harlow suggests that this behavior in the monkey results directly from a primary factor, an instinctive contact-comfort mechanism (a term he borrows from Bowlby, 1958). By comparison and inference, this phenomenology, mediated by IRM's in the monkey, has a counterpart in what we see dynamically, adaptionally, and economically in the human infant in the concept of normal developmental symbiosis (Mahler, 1952).

---

[18]We cannot be certain that Harlow's "true" affectional bonds in monkeys is the equivalent of the libidinal object of psychoanalysis.

COMMENTS

These observations suggest that the variation in maturation of neonates of given species, i. e., the degree of altriciality or precocity, determines the level of importance for a given organism of dependence on the object. The more altricial the organism, the more will dependence become a central factor in its earliest life experiences and adaptions. And the more this dependence on the object will become a factor influencing the character of psychic development in that particular organism.

State of Differentiation at Birth and the Instinctual Drives

However, this variation of neonatal state does not influence the fact that in all species, precocial or altricial, the instinctual drives, specifically the libidinal ones, are or become largely dependent on the object for gratification. We do not mean by this that, in the human child libido is object-seeking at birth. As Jacobson (1964) and Spitz (1965b) observe, the instinctual drives, as well as self and object representations, are not differentiated in the human newborn; but, object libido differentiates out eventually in all species where libido or a drive of this type exists.

Freud (1920) stated the ultimate aim of Eros to be the unification of two organisms and thereby the insurance of reproduction and perpetuation of the species. Eros is an instinctual force existing in all species that require both sexes for reproduction. Whatever the species' evolutionary pattern of adaptation, its preservation is guaranteed by the development of object relations. And evolution insures the development of in-species object relations by directing sexual impulses to an object, i. e., by the structuring of object libido.

It seems plausible from ethological observations, that there are many species lower than man in the phylogenetic scale in which an instinctual drive corresponding to libido in man is sufficiently differentiated to be object-seeking at birth. It is our impression that the phenomenon of imprinting and the attachment of Harlow's monkeys to inanimate object-like "things" can be explained on that basis. We do not shy away from using the term "libido-like" in attributing instinctual drives to organisms of a phylogenetic level other than man's. Lorenz (1953, p. 117) suggests that animals experience phenomena the nature of which are akin to those that pertain to man. And Freud (1940) proposed that a notable degree of psychic organization, including the development of a superego, probably occurs in animals that resemble man mentally (p. 147).

State of Differentiation at Birth
and the Mechanisms of Object-Attachment

Those precocial organisms[19] that imprint demonstrate a sufficient degree of maturation of cognitive and executive apparatuses to perceive gestalts, if only grossly as Hess (1959) suggests, and can, even within minutes after birth, effect an independent motoric approach to the mother. The importance of these responses to the organism's adaptation cannot be underestimated. Lorenz, Hess and others (see Hess, 1959) have reported the long-lasting, irreversible

[19]Lorenz (1935, 1953) has made it clear, as has Hess (1959), that not all precocial young exhibit imprinting to nonspecies objects.

effects of imprinting and suggest what would appear to be the nature of that innate mechanism: to insure attachment to the object of the species and consequently the preservation of the species. Nor can the hazard that this mechanism presents be underestimated. A mal-imprinted subject would be of no service to its species. Indeed, as Liddell's experiments on twin goats indicate, reliance on such mechanisms may be hazardous because of the rigidity of patterning they impose.

Hess (1959) cited the remarkable responsiveness of the precocial neonate to the first gestalt it encounters by demonstrating that the natural mother is ignored in favor of the imprinted gestalt even after the period for imprinting has passed. If no exposure during the critical period for imprinting takes place, the natural mother is accepted. Thus Hess also has shown that even in the precocial organism mechanisms other than imprinting go into the formation of object relations, a fact which is not surprising. Our point here is that, as the term indicates, the "precocial" young, because of its greater degree of differentiation at birth is equipped with instinctively-activated mechanisms of relating to the object and is more independent than the altricial young. We postulate, then, that the anaclitic character of object relations in the precocial organisms (more than in the altricial young) is determined more directly from birth by the principle of Eros.

Spitz (1965b) describes the gradual, progressively differentiating processes of cognition in the altricial creature par excellence. Our present knowledge indicates that the human infant advances from the inability to perceive external gestalts, by the interlocking (Lorenz, 1935, 1953, p. 116) of innate and learning processes, to the gradual integration of such gestalts and, with the emergence of affects and the differentiation of the drives, to valuation of the object.

Here, too, certain innate instinctive factors (IRMs) seem to contribute to the processes that insure the development of object relations, as seen in the undifferentiated smiling response (Spitz 1965). But at birth, as with the cat and the dog, the human young is sufficiently helpless that unless the mother does a great deal of caring for it, it will die. This circumstance leads to the simple proposition that the altricial young is dependent and will not survive without maternal care, whereas the precocial young, as Harlow (1962, 1966) proposed, may suffer socially without it, but may well survive. Freud (1926), speaking of the human infant said,

> [Man] is sent into the world in a less finished state. As a result, the influence of the real external world upon it is intensified. . . . Moreover, the dangers of the external world have a greater importance for it, so that the value of the object which can alone protect it against them and take the place of its former intrauterine life is enormously enhanced. The biological factor, then, establishes the earliest situation of danger and creates the need to be loved which will accompany the child through the rest of its life [pp. 154-155].

We believe that it is just this fact, that *altriciality imposes dependence* to a far greater degree than does precocity, that may have led Harlow (1962, 1966) to comment on the role of mothers in the monkey. He noted that in the rhesus macaque, instinctive attachment to a cloth "doll" can be effected and that this "thing" or "doll" can then become valued as an "object" (Hess [1959] did a similar type of experiment in imprinting a "thing" [decoy] which became "object" by this instinctive attachment process). The cloth object could serve Harlow's monkey as a protector against fear. Because the neonate rhesus monkey could also accept, as an object to cling to, an infant as young as itself, Harlow (1962) observed that mothers were not essential for "normal" development in this relatively precocial organism. He suggested that mates (peers) were more important for the development of socialization and mating [20] (p. 138). He later (1966, pp. 268, 271) retracted his statement on the unimportance of mothers to rhesus infants. Harlow, we believe, made his initial observation with some foundation, albeit on limited observation, because the rhesus macaque is significantly more precocial than man and the role of instinctive attachment behavior seems to be much greater in this species than it is in man. *Attachment of the human neonate to any object is not possible, IRM's notwithstanding, precisely because of the immaturity of his cognitive and executive apparatuses and the nondifferentiation of his instinctual drives.*

Primary Socialization: Imprinting and the
Undifferentiated Smiling Response

Or we might approach the problem from another angle. Can we apply to man Scott's (1963) postulate that primary socialization occurs as a general phenomenon in the animal kingdom? When Scott proposed that the smiling response in the human infant was indicative of primary socialization (p. 23), he suggested that instinctive and acquired factors operate to achieve this process (p. 4). However, we have the impression that in his view imprinting is the paradigm for primary socialization and that the source of this socialization is dominantly instinctive. As Scott

[20]The importance of peers for the development of object relations might have been overestimated by Harlow, but is often underestimated in psychoanalytic theory. Jacobson (1964) has drawn attention to this factor with reference to identification.

noted, Gray (1958) asserts that the smiling response is the equivalent of the following response that occurs in imprinting, and that it is an index of imprinting in man.

We are in accord with one fundamental issue in the concept put forth by Scott, that is, his proposal that both imprinting and the processes that effect the undifferentiated smiling response insure the preservation of the species by setting down the nucleus of the representation of the object specific for the species. Imprinting, according to Lorenz and Hess leads to the subsequent attachment of the sexual impulses to the object (the species) to which the organism is imprinted. Psychosexual theory and the concepts of libidinization of the object suggest a similar construct: the sexual impulses are first experienced in relation to the object of first affectional attachment.

We concur then that some kind of primary socialization occurs in man. But significant differences exist, we believe, between imprinting and the smiling response. The first of these has reference to the character of their emergence. According to Lorenz and Hess, imprinting is a special case of conditioning, is not associative learning and is the product of an IRM activated by a stimulus of specific-enough characteristics. It is a global response that partakes of large motoric and affective components, all the result of a sufficiently-differentiated CNS. The classical imprinting to which we refer occurs within hours after birth, is unrelated to prior experience with an object and takes place independently of whether or not the activity released by the stimulus is functional (Lorenz, 1953, p. 115).

The undifferentiated smiling response (Spitz, 1946a, 1965b), on the other hand, emerges six to twelve weeks after birth, tends to have a more specific affective component than occurs in imprinting and has little specific motor response associated with it, other than the activity of the facial musculature. One finds, not an abrupt onset that turns on as by a light switch, but rather a certain equivocation, a hesitancy; one can almost postulate the infant's effort to sort out the perceptual field with a now-on, now-off smiling response. This gives way, within days, to the more reliable, unequivocal undifferentiated smile to the face-gestalt. The same "gradualness" characterizes the evolving of that undifferentiated response into the now-on, now-off selective smile and the stranger responses, and then to the stabilized differentiated smile and the predictable separation anxiety and stranger response. This last occurs at about the sixth month and indicates that the specific libidinal object has emerged. We agree with Spitz (1965b) that this gradual development is in the nature of a learning process.

We assume that the IRM which releases the undifferentiated smile (Spitz, 1965b, p. 95) interlocks with learning, the latter being made possible by the differentiating capacity to perceive the stimulus (face-gestalt) that activates the IRM. In other words, the IRM is anaclitic; it is contingent on ego functioning and must, therefore, be more subject to the vicissitudes of ego development in the altricial organism than where the ego is significantly more differentiated at birth. For example, we assume that if the stimulus cannot be perceived, the IRM will not be activated. Spitz (1965b) postulates that the gradual sorting out of the face-gestalt from the more amorphous and broader gratification-gestalt is influenced by the mother-child interaction— indeed, that the meaningfulness of the face-gestalt emerges from that interaction. We propose here that this process is the result of altriciality, and that experience and learning influence development (in Hartmann's sense) as the CNS differentiation lag is taken up by postnatal maturation. It is our impression then, that the IRM which sets off the undifferentiated smiling response is an instinctive structure that serves primary socialization, but it is activated by the *experiential valuation* of the face-percept, an ever-present part percept of the total gratification-gestalt.

The second difference between imprinting and the undifferentiated smiling response has to do with differences in drive characteristics. For the present we assume that imprinting is fueled by an instinctual drive which is object-seeking at the time of activation of the response. Since imprinting occurs at or near birth, such drive must be object-seeking at or near birth. It is not unreasonable to hypothesize such early differentiation of drives in precocial organisms which are able to effect an instinctively monitored object attachment so soon after birth.

Recent psychoanalytic theory assumes that instinctual drive in man is undifferentiated at birth (Jacobson, 1964; Spitz, 1965b). Much consensus exists among psychoanalysts that no object libido is present at birth; well-known exceptions are the Balints (1953) and Fairbairn (1954). And from our own observations of infants, we find no evidence of object-libido. We therefore doubt that imprinting as described by Lorenz and Hess occurs in man, and we say with certainty that in man it cannot occur at or near birth.

When does object libido differentiate in man? *Phenomenologically*, one might postulate a component of libido that is object-seeking to emerge when the undifferentiated smile appears, and to fuel the IRM that releases the smile response. What psychical energy could fuel such object-related behavior? Could object libido begin to differentiate now? At the time of the emergence of the undifferentiated smiling response, primary narcissism differentiates as the infant perceives that help comes from outside its body-ego boundaries (Mahler, 1952, 1967). What is outside that boundary, however, is not yet libidinally perceived as outside the self. Present opinion would be that libido has no power of attachment to an object at this time; under the dominance of primary narcissism, that seeming object libido remains attached to the self because the object-in-sight is but a part of self (Mahler, 1952, 1965, 1967; Spitz, 1950, 1965b; Parens, 1970a). The most we can say at present is that with the undifferentiated smile, a narcissistic cathexis—the forerunner of an object cathexis—is sent out to the face representation and that neither cathexis nor representation survive the period of actual face presentation. That is to say, the face-gestalt representation is not retained in memory because the cathexis of that representation is unstable, and withdrawn when the object is out of sight. We view the differentiation in libido that takes place at this time as a transitional step from "absolute primary narcissism" (Mahler, 1967, 1968b) to object libido. We assume that the object is perceived and libidinized as part of self, and remains so until the appearance of separation anxiety, which tells us that the perception of the object as not-part-of-self has now occurred. The consensus among analysts (A. Freud, 1947, 1954; Jacobson, 1954, 1964; Mahler, 1952, 1965, 1968b; Spitz, 1950, 1965b; and others) is that object libido will not make its appearance in the human until the phase of the libidinal object and the appearance of separation anxiety, until the beginning of separation-individuation, in Mahler's terms.

Thus, we suggest that significant differences exist in the nature of the emergence of imprinting in precocial organisms as compared to the emergence of the undifferentiated smiling response in humans. In addition, we believe that each response is fueled by instinctual drive energy that is in a different state of differentiation. We do believe, however, that the two responses effect the same important task: both imprinting and the undifferentiated smile serve the process of primary socialization and of inscribing indelibly in the psyche the nucleus of the representation of the object of the species. Their inherent differences undoubtedly lie, in part, in the degree of differentiation of each species at birth.

The Period of Insufficient Somatopsychic Differentiation

We have suggested, then, that the relative immaturity of the altricial organism is determined by that organism's phylogenetic pattern of terminating its fetal state prior to the development of sufficient functioning to effect potential neonatal instinctive patterns of attachment seen in certain precocial animals. We call the lag period during which such functional capacity emerges the *period of insufficient somato-psychic differentiation* (Spitz uses the term *nondifferentiation*, applying it specifically to psychic organization). Back-tracking a bit, we ask: can such a period of insufficient differentiation have obliterated, phylogenetically, phenomena such as imprinting, which follow on the heels of parturition? It would seem that the *gradual differentiation* of cognitive (as well as affective and executive) functioning *out-of-utero* has made learning operative to a greater degree in the development of attachment to the object in the altricial young. For the altricial young, the impact of external gestalts is minimal, or at least less imperative, at birth, and these gestalts cannot be rapidly brought to bear on an exquisitely sensitive, "ready for work" memory apparatus. How well Spitz has described the gradual sorting out from a myriad of external stimuli: "a meaningful entity from a universe of meaningless things" (1965b, p. 96). During such a period of insufficient differentiation, much happens that is in accordance with Schneirla's observations and hypothesis: that maturation and experience factors are "inextricably interrelated in individual development" (Rosenblatt et al., 1962, p. 199).

The variance in the status of maturation of the newborn of a given species, then, influences the complemental series of innate, instinctive factors versus acquired, learned factors, in the development of object relations. Schur (1960) believes (in agreement with Lorenz) that phylogenetically, under the impact of selective evolution, curtailment of instinctive behavior and development of acquired, learned, "insightful" behavior go hand in hand. There is then a shift to the right in the equation "innate vs. acquired," determined in part by the neonatal period of insufficient differentiation. Spitz (1965b, p. 9) reminds us that Freud formulated this complemental series with reference to neurosis in 1905 and later in 1937: that congenital (innate, instinctive) factors interact with environmental (experiential, acquired, learned) factors in determining the emergence of neurosis. Spitz notes that it applies to all such biological phenomena. Accepting this basic principle, we address ourselves specifically to man's anaclitic beginnings.

Adaptation to Altriciality

Because evolutionary adjustment results in adaptation not so much on the part of the neonate as of his parents, we postulate that innate attachment responses become less all-important in the altricial neonate. The young's helplessness places it in a state of utter dependence, and, indeed, *adaptation to altriciality is dependence.* That dependence is expressed, when there is sufficient differentiation of cognitive and affective functioning, in the state of symbiosis formulated by Mahler (1952, 1963, 1965, 1968b).

In Spitz's view, the infant's psychological organization develops at about six months of age (1960), allowing for the development of object relations as we know them in man. It has been generally assumed that this is also the time when the ego achieves a given degree of autonomy from the id, in the id-ego differentiation that Freud (1940) spoke of, and on which Hartmann et al., (1939 onward) have significantly elaborated. Spitz recently (1965b) suggested that the ego emerges in differentiation from the id at about three months of age, i. e., that diacritic perceptual function, cognition, and affective structures emerge at this period. Mahler (1968a) has agreed with this timing and has placed the beginning of the normal symbiotic phase at the same time. Pulling these recent formulations together, we might say that when the human infant becomes aware of psychic events—is psychically born, so to speak—, he is in the symbiotic phase. *He begins his conscious psychic life in a state of psychologic dependence on the object.*

Dependence, the earliest state of adaptation in man, profoundly influences the development of his psychic organization, a point Freud (1923, 1926, 1940) made repeatedly and one that Mahler (1952, through 1968b) has already greatly extended in her formulations of normal symbiosis and separation-individuation. The human ego in its cradle is an anaclitic ego and uses the mother as its auxiliary ego (Spitz, 1965b). The child's biological dependence on the mother, so integral to its need-gratification experiences, early becomes charged with affect and therewith acquires a psychological character. The stamp of that ontogeny remains. At the level of phylogeny where we find man, and largely by the fact of these altricial beginnings, we agree with Lichtenstein (1961), that man exists in an essentially symbiotic life-condition.

SUMMARY

We have attempted to formulate the thesis that the more altricial an organism, the greater will be the influence of dependence as a psychological force in its adaptation and in the development of its object relations.

The greater the degree of altriciality, the less the degree of psychophysiologic differentiation at birth. We have proposed that if man is indeed the altricial creature par excellence, then he experiences a longer neonatal period of insufficient somatopsychic differentiation than other organisms, a period during which the significant lag of his maturation is made up. This condition influences psychic development on two counts:

1. The longer the period of insufficient differentiation —as a result of which phylogenetically inherent instinctive attachment mechanisms (IRMs) could not be activated— the greater the influence of experience.

2. The metapsychological and phenomenological aspects of protracted helplessness make the need for the object explicit.

The first proposition suggests that altriciality is one of the factors that pushes the complemental series equation, 'innate vs. acquired,' to the right. It would then follow that in the early psychic development of an altricial organism, in contrast to a precocial one, the influence of instinctive structures is lessened while that of experience is increased.

As we focus on the nature of psychic experiences in early life, we see that in man, the infant's biologic helplessness and dependence soon determine an intense valuation of the object, and a profound psychologic dependence on that object erupts. And we observe that the differentiations of the ego and the superego, of the self, of the object, and of object relations, have their beginnings in the experiential gestalt of *dependence on the object.*

3. Inner Sustainment

INTRODUCTION

By virtue of its genetic pre-eminence and its long duration, the childhood dependence of man is an important
determinant in the epigenesis of personality development
and has a developmental line which Anna Freud has
sketched: "from dependency to emotional self-reliance
and adult object relationships" (1963, p. 247).

Of course, age-appropriate dependence in the adult is
not the same as it is in the child. As the individual develops, he moves from one condition of dependence to another, a result of the evolving character of his needs and his
changing object cathexes. Thus, within the framework of
an anaclitic life-condition, he progresses from beginnings
of helplessness to a position of self-reliance wherein he can
determine the means by which to gratify his recurring
needs. There is in this line of development a complemental
series: dependence vs. self-reliance. We see an economic
condition that determines the equilibrium of this complemental equation: The degree to which one is self-reliant is

largely determined by the stability of what we have called libidinal *inner sustainment* (Saul, 1970; Parens, 1970b). Inner sustainment reflects the state of the organism's libidinal economy which results from the interplay of the psychic forces within him. That is, it derives from the dynamic and economic states within the psychic organization that lead to feeling loved and supported from within. The degree to which one is libidinally sustained from within is reflected by the degree to which one is free from the need for sustainment from without.

METAPSYCHOLOGICAL NOTES

The Psychic Representation

Saul (1970) describes a patient "internally sustained by the continuance in his mind, in his feelings, his self-image, his relations with others . . . of the love, confidence, and tolerance of his mother during his early years. In contrast, others with every external advantage but with a lack of parental sustenance in early life remain unsustained in facing even the most protected lives" (p. 222).

Of pertinence here is Freud's (1923) observation: "[T]he effects of the first identifications made in earliest childhood will be general and lasting" (p. 31). And similarly, Mahler has spoken of the residua of the mother-child relationship that remain at the core of the psychic life of the organism (Mahler, 1965; Mahler and Furer, 1963). Novey (1958) addresses himself most directly to this thesis: the subject's "inner experiences of . . . objects [i.e., their psychic representations] is . . . of prime significance in determining . . . his degree of internal comfort" (p. 60).

The *psychic representation* may be understood as Sandler et al. (1962, 1963) describe it, as a modifiable schema constructed over time out of a multitude of impressions, images, affects, and events. It is the mental representation of the world, both inner and outer, as perceived by the subject. There are representations of objects, of self, and of psychic experience. These are represented as they are perceived, with affective coloring, within an action context, and with varying degrees of cathexis. The psychic representation is a *product* and not a process (see Waelder, 1937, p. 418).

The processes which introduce the representations into the psychic organization—internalization—(Hartmann and Loewenstein, 1962) and which act upon and integrate these representations—identification and introjection—into psychic structure and self-concepts, we may call here the *assimilative* processes (Brody and Mahoney, 1964; see also Sandler, 1960).

Genetic and Structural Considerations

Inner sustainment arises from two roots: primary narcissism and the object relation. Primary narcissism leaves its nucleus in inner sustainment, as it does, of course, in self-esteem (Freud, 1914). In normal development, however, the rigors of the reality principle soon undermine that narcissism salutarily and enhance the development of object cathexes and object relations. The initial experiences of separation anxiety deal primary narcissism and infantile omnipotence a significant blow. Each succeeding experience of separation anxiety conveys to the child that he is nigh-totally sustained from without, and his dependence—his psychologic dependence—is suddenly at its peak. From here on, the object relation influences evolving of inner sustainment by the developments the former in-

duces in the psychic apparatus. It is our impression that
the object cathexis is by far the chief contributor to mature inner sustainment.

Basic trust (Erikson, 1959),[1] an ego quality derived
from earliest object relations, is fundamental to inner sustainment. The term is the equivalent of "confidence" used
earlier by Benedek (1956). Erikson proposes that basic
trust or mistrust is the outcome of the psychosocial crisis
of the first year of life. If early life experiences include a
large dose (Fries, 1946) of interactions with competent,
loving, realistically tolerant parents who respect the indi-
viduality of the child, the psychic representations of the
parents, the self, and the experiences will generally have
these characteristics (Benedek, 1949, 1956); and basic
trust evolves. If such experiences have been largely hostile
and ungratifying, the internal representations will have the
corresponding characteristics, and basic trust will be poor.

Internalization of object relations is essential to two
major interrelated developmental processes that lead to inner sustainment and self-reliance: (1) separation-individuation, and (2) the differentiation of psychic structure.

1. *Separation-Individuation.* The sense of basic trust is
important to the child's capacity to accept the reality that
the omnipotent symbiosis with the mother cannot be
maintained and that she cannot always sustain him exter-
nally. As Erikson (1959) remarks: "It is against the ...
impressions of having been deprived, ... divided ... aban-

---

[1] In defining basic trust, Erikson (1959) remarks with regard to "trust":
"what is commonly implied in reasonable trustfulness [of] ... others ...
and a simple sense of trustworthiness as far as oneself is concerned" (p. 56).
With reference to "basic," he means that it is not "especially conscious" (p.
56). And also: "The general state of trust ... implies not only that one has
learned to rely on the sameness and continuity of the outer providers but
also that one may trust oneself and the capacity of one's own organs to
cope with urges; that one is able to consider oneself trustworthy enough so
that the providers will not need to be on guard or to leave" (p. 61).

doned, . . . that basic trust must be established and maintained" (pp. 60-61).

Mahler and her coworkers have further elaborated this process by their observations and formulations of separation-individuation (Mahler, 1963, 1965, 1968b; Mahler and Furer, 1963; Pine and Furer, 1963). Progressive schematization and stabilization of object representations make possible, and lead to, object constancy (Hartmann, 1952; Mahler, 1961, 1963, 1965, 1968b), i. e., to stable mental representations of the love object who is thus not lost to the ego, nor to the self, when the object is physically absent. The ego sustained from within by the "good" object representation, further secures its quality of basic trust and advances individuation. The separation-individuation phase achieves its goal with the attainment of object constancy (Mahler, 1961, 1965) and the beginning of self constancy (Jacobson, 1964). Identification with object representations is particularly relevant to the stabilization of self-representations and, from there, to identity formation. Both object constancy, with stable *object* representations, and beginning self constancy and identity formation, with stabilizing *self*-representations, facilitate the process of individuation. More and more sustained from within. The child can separate more and more from the external objects. Both object and self-constancy are nuclear to inner sustainment.

2. *Differentiation of Psychic Structure.* In 1923, Freud formulated the importance of introjection and identifications to the differentiation of the ego. We have already reviewed some of his views on this most important hypothesis (see Chapter 1): the genetic relevance of object relations and the assimilative processes to structural differentiation. We emphasize here the importance of the qualities

of object relations and of psychic representations which, by assimilation into structure, act upon and influence the ego's inherent tendencies.

Freud also noted (1923) that the superego differentiates from the ego by "the forming of a precipitate in the ego" consisting of the identifications with both the mother and the father (p. 34). These identifications, "the representative of our relations to our parents" (p. 36), provide models and patterns for the critical, moral functions of the superego, those of the loving, supportive superego and those of the ego ideal.

In line with these formulations, we suggest two relations of the assimilation into psychic structure of early objectal experiences *vis-à-vis* the quality of inner sustainment: (1) The patterns and qualities of parental interactions with the self are taken into the ego and superego and will appear in the character of the functions of that ego and superego. Thus, for the usual child with average maturational and developmental capacity, *the degree and quality to which he was sustained from without by his parents will, by internalization and assimilation, become the degree and quality to which he is sustained from within.* (2) Ego and superego developments are influenced by objects in proportion to the degree that object relations are cathected. Poor libidinization of the object leads to unstable identifications, and these contribute less than optimally to ego and superego development, thereby impoverishing inner sustainment. In addition, whatever the quality of the object as libidinal object (whether "good" or "bad") *poor cathexis* of an object leads to deficits in the progression from primary narcissism to object libido and secondary narcissism. This deficit robs the subject of the gratification of object love, a significant and more progressive source of inner sustainment and self-esteem than residual primary narcissism. It also robs the psychic apparatus of potential developments.

Briefly then, the basic characteristics of the ego, as well as of the superego, are determined in their development, to a greater or lesser degree, by the nature of the internal representations as these are assimilated into psychic structure. We assume, on the other hand, that the young ego does, to some extent, determine the character of the introjection and identification processes and their results—at first by its own inherent givens and limitations (Freud, 1923, 1937a; Hartmann, 1939, 1950) and then, as the ego develops, by its own tendencies and capabilities to accept or reject certain experiences and object characteristics. With further differentiation of psychic structure, assimilation of new internal representations and identifications—although not necessarily new objects—continues, and, with the advent of latency, the architectural framework of the psychic organization is established. Much, however, is yet to impinge on that structure: new life events, new object relations, massive upsurges of libidinal drives, remarkable development of ego functioning and ego skills. Changes in internal representations prevail well into adulthood and continue to modify the intrapsychic agencies (Abraham, 1925; Freud, 1921, 1940; Waelder, 1937; Novey, 1958) and resultant inner sustainment.

The degree of inner sustainment depends upon the level of development of the psychic organization. There is an age-adequate (A. Freud, 1962, 1963) range of feeling sustained from within in balance with the expectation of sustainment from without. In addition, inner sustainment is subject to regression depending on the stresses that impinge on the psychic organization, on its areas of specific vulnerability (Saul, 1947; Saul and Lyons, 1952) coming from the drives and the environment.

Dynamic and Adaptive Considerations

The psychic apparatus functions and develops at all times under the influence of the principle of multiple function (Waelder, 1930). At a given point in time, the simultaneous dynamic functioning of the ego and superego in interaction with psychic content factors, i.e., psychic representations and identity formations, will yield the quality of inner sustainment.

Viewing the functions of the ego[2] in terms of adaptation to internal and external environments best clarifies the importance of its role in the development and maintenance of inner sustainment. As the individual grows, he develops more and more the skills to cope. With age-adequate development of ego functions (Beres, 1956)—of the sense of reality; the capability to cathect and to retain object relations; to control instinctual drives; to develop thought and communication; to enhance the development of autonomous functions and master cognitive and motoric tasks; to develop integrative capabilities of his psychic apparatus—the organism acquires the conscious and preconscious sense that he can increasingly count on himself for mastery of danger situations, for solving problems and overcoming obstacles. Within those areas where he repeatedly experiences successful mastery, he develops a greater degree of autonomous capability and competence.

The converse: repeated experiences of excessive anxiety, of inability to modify anxiety-producing situations, leads not only to feelings of insecurity and vulnerability, but also to expenditures of psychic energies for insuffi-

[2]We suspect that constitutionally defective ego apparatuses are less capable of internalization and identification processes that approximate reasonably actual life events, than are ego apparatuses that function normally.

ciently effective purposes. The individual whose ego cannot cope with the problems of adaptation will perforce
seek shelter by turning to objects or substitutes not always
more competent than himself, or he will set up defenses
that lead to symptom formation and relative libidinal depletion. Thus, the sense of autonomy and competence that
comes with satisfactory development of the ego is central
to feeling sustained from within: It makes it possible for
the individual to use his own emotional as well as functional resources.

The role of the superego, too, is prominent in inner
sustainment. As in the danger situation series, fear of loss
of the superego's love (from latency on) is a nodal source
of anxiety, directly influencing the economy of the libido.
Generally, the challenging of superego dictates leads to
guilt. And whereas guilt can be a strong socializing factor
which limits antisocial behavior and encourages altruism, it
can also be disruptive of well-being. In terms of libido,
guilt leads to a withholding of love from the superego.
Eventually, inner sustainment is greatly influenced by the
character of the superego, being further assured if the superego (i. e., its introjects) is reasonably benevolent and
supportive. With structural differentiations of the latency-
age child, the quality and status of feeling internally sustained will depend largely on the harmony between the
ego and the superego as these stand in their relations to the
id and reality.

Achievements and goals for the self are determined by
idealized self-representations as they are influenced by
compromise formations between environmental expectations and the pressure of drive derivatives (Sandler, et al.,
1963). The ego ideal is progressively modified by identifications (Hammerman, 1965) and holds up to the ego
these compromise formations of the ideal self (Sandler, et

al., 1963). Discrepancies between the ego ideal and the ego (Piers and Singer, 1953), "between the self-representation and the wishful concept of the self" (Jacobson, 1964, p. 131) determine the status of self-esteem. Self-esteem, in turn, as first described by Freud (1914) is a store of self-directed libidinal supplies. It is a supply of love from within, then, and is therefore a prime contributor to the status of inner sustainment.

Formation and stabilization of psychic representations in the child lead to the ability to survive without undue anxiety in the absence of the mother. The child can now be alone in "external" reality, as the ego holds self-and object representations within (Winnicott, 1965). We have noted that those processes leading to separation-individuation significantly determine the character of identity formations. It is important that identity formations be ego syntonic in order to not create chronic anxiety. Thus they must conform to superego demands or they will create guilt; they must also conform to the standards of the ego ideal or they will induce shame. The more stable optimal identity formations, the more assured sustainment from within. Of course, the sense of self depends on the value the objects place on the subject. Then, in later development, if one has a reasonable degree of self-value, one tends to trust one's judgement, decisions, and ideas.

Holding in perspective epigenetic evolving of the psychic organization and age-adequate functioning, the degree to which the ego is sustained from within makes it more or less capable of dealing with internal and external realities self-reliantly. With optimal inner sustainment, deprivations and hazards can be met with optimal stability, and the ego can set itself maximally to the task of adaptation. Speaking dynamically and economically, the better the degree of sustainment from within, the less the dependence for sup-

port on external sources. With inner sustainment transiently overtaxed, as by the presence of a vulnerability-
specific stress (Saul and Lyons, 1952), the ego reacts with
fight or flight (Saul, 1951) often regressing to earlier patterns of dependence by turning to external sources for the
support it transiently does not have from within.

Thus, some of the contributions—arising from object
relations—to the dynamics of inner sustainment are as follows:

The character of inner sustainment derives from the
qualities and stability of internal representations and from
the continuing effects of assimilative processes on these.
With satisfactory basic trust, self constancy and object
constancy, one is sustained from within and can be alone.
Identity formations are determined largely by the stabilization of object- and self-representations. Stabilization of optimal identity formations in turn adds significantly to the
quality of inner sustainment. Good, stable, internal representations and identifications influence the inherent character of ego functioning. With optimal experiences of mastery and resulting autonomy and competence of the ego,
self-reliance and inner sustainment follow. Age-adequate
ego functioning, of itself, adds to sustainment from within
by guaranteeing a closer approximation to ego-ideal function and by the narcissistic gain that accompanies mastery
of tasks. (See Freud, 1914, regarding the second source of
self-regard.) The status of self-esteem resulting from the
harmony between ego-ideal components and the self-representations is a direct contributor to sustainment from
within. The object representations assimilated by introjection and identification give the superego the qualities of
its varied functions. From latency on, the fear of loss of
love from the superego is a prime determinant of anxiety
and significantly influences that status of inner sustain-

ment. A reasonable, supportive superego fortifies inner sustainment.

The dynamic state then resulting from the character of these psychic constructs and structural functions comes largely from the influence of internalization of the object relations upon the constitutional givens of the individual. This brings to mind Rene Dubos' (1967) apt reminder that the environment determines the phenotypic expression of our genotypic endowment.

SUMMARY

A central process at work in the development from dependence to self-reliance is internalization of object relations. Through this process, as the child was sustained by the objects during his long childhood, he progressively is more or less sustained from within. The better libidinally sustained from within, the less dependent on external sources for emotional support.

As the individual develops, there is an equilibrium and a general progression to the right in the equation: dependence vs. self-reliance. We propose that along with age-adequate development of psychic functioning, libidinal inner sustainment determines the shift of that equation. Inner sustainment is subject to regression, depending upon the degree of psychic stress. The stability of the representational, structural, and identity constructs will determine the stability of inner sustainment and its resistance to regression. In the average human—and in some other species too—the more optimal the earliest object relations, the greater the stability of object cathexes and the better developed and stable are all the factors leading to libidinal inner sustainment.

Contributions to the quality of inner sustainment come from interrelated sources within the psychic organization.

1. The residual infantile narcissism (and omnipotence).

2. The quality and degree of development of primary autonomous ego functioning to age-adequate competence which contributes to self-confidence, to the character of identity formations and to individuation.

3. The internalization of object relations. In this context, the *characteristics of psychic representations* as well as the character of *assimilations of these representations* into the psychic organization are of central importance.

These profoundly influence:

a. The character of structural differentiation, of structural functioning and content (Hartmann and Loewenstein, 1962).

b. The status of separation-individuation (Mahler 1963, 1965, 1968b) which evolves epigenetically about the nuclear elements of basic trust, self-object differentiations, self- and object-constancy and identity formations; and,

c. The presence of residual infantile intrapsychic conflict, particularly ego—superego tensions leading to shame and/or guilt with resultant loss of self-esteem and/or threat of loss of love from the superego (Piers and Singer, 1953; Hammerman, 1965).

4. Two Co-ordinates of Dependence

INTRODUCTION

In delineating the line of development from dependence to self-reliance, we find it useful to consider dependence in terms of its constituents. We see dependence as being composed of two interacting elements of equal importance, in other words, co-ordinates. One is dependent *on* an object *for* the gratification of a need; one is dependent *on* someone *for* something. Each co-ordinate undergoes modifications: cathexes of objects shift according to the source and character of gratifications, while at the same time the needs are undergoing evolution. Each co-ordinate significantly influences the other. Certain needs become object-specific, and certain objects induce modes of behavior characteristic for certain needs. Thus, a three-year-old may be clinging, demanding, afraid of electric plugs when he is with his mother, but not when with his sister or a stranger.

135

DEPENDENCE ON THE OBJECT—"ON WHOM"

Early in analytic formulations, Abraham (1924) and Freud (1905, 1926, 1933, etc.) pointed to the importance of the vicissitudes of object relations in conjunction with the sequential phases of psychosexual development. The conditions created by instinctual demands and the child's utter helplessness make it essential that help come from without.

The degree to which the human child is incapable of bringing about gratification of needs *by his own actions* pertains to dependence "on the object." We may assume for the present that the capacity to bring about gratification of needs begins in a response context (IRMs, reflex mechanisms), where disturbance in homeostasis leads to reactive discharge and signaling such as crying which brings the mother into action. In the beginning, the infant's "action" is biophysiologic. But as psychic structure develops, adaptational capacity and activity enable the child to become progressively free from dependence on a specific object. Then if he does not find gratification in one place, he can seek it in another or can deal with his needs in a variety of adaptive ways. Man's capacity to effect and insure by his own actions the gratification of his needs, reaches its peak in middle adulthood and declines to the degree that aging processes diminish his freedom of motility and his capacity for self-care, and as object losses occur with greater frequency. Jones (1957), for example, remarked that as he was aging, Freud despised being dependent on someone to open a window for him.

All humans are more or less bound to an object other than the self for the gratification of many of their needs. Freud (1915) observed that some instincts are capable of autoerotic satisfaction whereas "those sexual instincts which from the outset require an object, and the needs of the ego-instincts, . . . are never capable of auto-erotic satisfaction" (pp. 134-135). The editors of Freud's works, comment on "the existence of auto-erotic libidinal instincts . . . [and] *non-auto-erotic* libidinal and self-preservative instincts" that are satisfied by parental care. Schur's (1953) statement is relevant: "We can master internal danger only indirectly by mastery of the environment; i. e., we can provide food or find a sex partner" (p. 84). In short then, man can gratify some of his needs autoerotically, but the gratification of many others requires an object.

We see several factors that evolve in the line of development from dependence to emotional self-reliance: (1) the development of ego autonomy and competence; (2) shifts in object-libido and cathexes; and (3) the status of "inner sustainment" (see Chapter 3).

(1) The organism passes from utter helplessness to the acquisition of ego skills which can effect the gratification of his needs—both autoerotic and nonautoerotic. In this sense, the child's dependence on objects is inversely related to the maturation and development of the ego (the organ of adaptation—Hartmann, 1939, 1958).

(2) Object relations differentiate; modifications in priorities and in the character of the objects result from shifts in narcissistic and object libido as well as from displacements of object cathexes, as occurs (a) with the passage from the dyadic pregenital phases to the triadic phallic phase, to the latency phase, adolescence, and young adulthood under the impetus of psychosexual development, and (b) from certain ubiquitous life events which activate differentiation of object relations, such as adventitious separations from parents, birth of a sibling, etc.; actual object losses also effect differentiation of object relations via dis-

placement of object cathexes and shifts in object/narcissistic libido; so will severe physical illness.

Principal Object Relations

The Child-Mother Relation: In 1926, Freud formulated that in the child-mother dyad lies the nucleus of the first danger-situation and the prime precipitant of separation anxiety. The mother is the first love-object for both sexes (Freud, 1926, 1940); by her functions as auxiliary ego and by her stimulation of erotogenic zones, she activates affectional and sensual libido. At the outset of life, the mother is also protector against trauma, both internal and external. She protects not only against over-riding libidinal impulses but aggressive ones as well.

The concept of symbiosis formulated by Mahler (1952 on; also commented upon by Benedek, 1956, and Jacobson, 1954), is based on this dyadic relation. Alpert (1959) and others base the concept of the "need-satisfying" object on the mother-child relation. Nearly all the writings with which we are acquainted model early child-parent phenomena on the child-mother dyad. This is true of Spitz, Mahler (who has, however, also drawn attention to the importance of the father; e.g., 1952), Jacobson, Bowlby, Benedek, the Balints, Ribble among others. Interestingly, Freud, who wrote extensively on the phallic phase of development, often focused on the child-father relation particularly because of its prominence in the Oedipus complex. Then, in 1926, with the formulation of the determinants of anxiety, the child-mother relation also came into prominence in his writings.

The Child-Father Relation: In Freud's writings, the pregenital aspects of the child-father dyad appear in 3 areas: in the formation of an affectional libidinal tie arising from the expectable "protection, care and indulgence" (1913a, 1926); in identification (1913a, 1921); and in the source of religious ideas (1927, 1930).

(1) The formation of the affectional pregenital tie to the father is important in its relation to guilt (1913a; see Chapter 1) and, more important still, in the contribution it makes to the resolution of the Oedipus complex (1913a; 1926, Chapters 4 and 7; see also Chapter 1).

(2) An early comment on the identification with the father appears in terms of devouring the totem animal (1913a). In 1921, it was in speaking of pregenital identification with the father that Freud pointed to the child's wishes to be like the admired father, to take his place everywhere in imitation of him. Then, during the phallic phase, the wish to displace the father is in ascendency. The progression during this latter phase is from the wish to-*be*-the-father, to (again) the wish to-*be-like*-the-father without displacing him (Hammerman, 1966); this progression is achieved with the working through of the Oedipus complex.

(3) A further function of the child-father relation appears in terms of "modern" religious beliefs. Freud (1927, 1930) drew attention to the paternal attributes of deity; "God, the Father." This dyadic and triadic relation also appeared in the tracing of the origins of totemism to the "father-complex" (1913a) (See this Chapter 1).

We just noted that the dyadic model has its prototype in the child-mother relation. We believe that the earliest child-father relation differs from the child-mother relation essentially in having a lesser degree of object-invested narcissistic libido. We doubt that object differentiation according to sex occurs prior say to 12 months; rather, preferential cathexis of the mother arises from her functions. As greater cognitive and libidinal differentiation occur, the cathectic valence of the parental objects in an "average expectable environment" (Hartmann, 1939) tends to equalize. This takes place, we believe, prior to the phallic phase of psychosexual development. Although each parent is looked to for "protection, care and indulgence," role differentiation occurs, each parent being looked to for certain functions. With the emergence of the phallic-sensual current of the libido, which is inherently object-directed, in accord with Eros, the dyadic object cathexes undergo significant modification which leads to the triadic object relation of the Oedipus complex.

There are, in addition, object relations with peers even in the very young child. The dyad with a sibling, which holds a lesser cathexis than that with the parents, is complicated by the fact that it is also a triadic relation *vis-à-vis* the mother. The first experiences of rivalry take place in this triad, but it is, of course, a rivalry of a very different character from that of the oedipal phase.

In latency the peer relation mounts in importance, and in late adolescence the peer cathexis will become the prime cathexis, containing amalgamations of sensual and affectional libido. Peer relations of a lesser cathectic order also occur in friendships. Some parent-substitute dyads are well known.

With parenthood, the relation to the children is added to the marital dyad. Object relations are perpetuated, and with them, the advancement of civilization.

At all times in man, the genetically pre-eminent *dyadic* model underlies many of the variations in object relations. Indeed, the aim of object relations in terms of the principle of Eros is the unification of two organisms.

Freud elucidated in *The Future of an Illusion* (1927) that man's residual archaic, infantile helplessness against the forces of nature, has led to the development of religious constructs which take their characteristics from the infant-parent relations. The characteristics of these constructs is complex. Their origin is discernable, however, in the archaic past of the subject. In a number of cultures, particularly in Western Culture, religious deity results from the externalization of archaic psychic representations of the parents. These become part of the psychic organization during earliest development, particularly during the period when omnipotent dyadic object relations were operative (see Chapter 1.)

Eros is also inherent in the concepts of object constancy and identification, in the sense that an intrapsychic "unification" between self and object occurs. In those processes, relative independence from the object obtains in reality when the internalization and "taking into the ego" of the psychic representation of that object is achieved with sufficient stability. Winnicott (1965) suggests that "the capacity to be alone" follows the experience of obtaining a "good enough" degree of object constancy. Metapsychologically, therefore, the capacity to be alone means to be alone with "stable enough" object representations.

The primacy and continued importance of the dyadic model of object relations arises from the indelibility of early experiences which occur in the context of the child-mother relation. It is around the third month of life, according to Spitz (1965b) and Mahler (1952, 1963, 1968b), that the differentiation of the libidinal object and the processes that will lead to separation-individuation begin, processes which carve the dyadic object relation out of narcissism. The dyad is then the model from which subsequent permutations of object relations derive. Of course, much continuity exists from this dyad to the triad of the phallic phase and to further "sets" of object relations. For example, the wish to possess the love object exclusively for oneself, to eliminate competitors—which arises out of narcissism—is central to both the dyadic and triadic type of relation.

DEPENDENCE FOR THE GRATIFICATION
OF NEEDS—"FOR WHAT"

Freud described "needs" as tension states experienced by the organism which, in accordance with the pleasure principle, decrease as the needs in question are gratified. In *The Ego and the Id*, Freud (1923) observes: "We can only suppose that later on object cathexes proceed from the id, *which feels erotic trends as needs*. The ego . . . becomes aware of the object-cathexes, and either acquiesces in them or tries to fend them off by the process of repression" (p. 29; italics added).

We emphasize the factor of dependence for something and on someone inherent in many need-gestalts. As Levy (1954) observed, "Needs cannot survive *in vacuo*. The outer and inner environments are concomitant parts of their function" (p. 67).

We have suggested (see Chapter 2) that the needs are at first physiological-instinctive and instinctual, and are governed by biological homeostatic mechanisms; that they acquire a psychological dimension with the emergence of cognitive and affective structures. They may be the product of imbalances in physiologic-psychic homeostasis or of external dangers impinging on the ego.

In undertaking to define man's needs, our prime interest is not to dissect them out one from another in great detail, but to demonstrate broad categories.

The Needs

For our present purposes we have divided these into three broad categories, bearing in mind that clear lines between them may not exist and that each influences the status of the others.

The *physiological* needs for such things as food, warmth, sleep—whatever is necessary for physical survival—are cyclic and perpetual. The *libidinal* needs are more complicated. They are manifest from the beginning of life, and they may be subdivided into *sensual* and *affectional* needs. Our third category, *ego-developmental* needs, are those wherein the child turns to the object for training, for help with development in motor coordination, in communication, for skills and for education.

It probably rarely happens that needs occur as phenomena that belong to just one of these categories. Behavior is overdetermined, and need-gratifications are complex. For example, ego-developmental needs, such as requiring help to learn to walk or speak, also carry with them proprioceptive and locomotor libidinal gratifications, as well as the satisfaction provided by parental approval for performing. Indeed, the anticipation of approval invariably is an incentive to making efforts to walk, to speak, etc. Pearson (1952) observes that children in school often make efforts to do well to please parents and teachers as much as to learn and gratify curiosity, a factor well-known but rejected by parents and teachers with lofty ideals of education.

Generally one group of needs is no more important than another to the total organism's psychologic survival. However, under particular circumstances, one need may predominate while carrying with it the gratification of others.

The hungry child is pressed by one aim: to gratify his hunger; but he also must be picked up, held appropriately, and be offered the nipple, inasmuch as his own ego cannot achieve these steps necessary to gratifying his oral needs. Or a toddler may run to his mother for protection against the onslaught of another child who is advancing on him with a raised shovel. He wants protection, not love. These various needs do not necessarily coincide in their aim; those which at the moment have the greatest motivating force or cathexis claim authority over the rest. Human behavior is often motivated by simultaneous and, at times, paradoxical needs. It is generally accepted that behavior is overdetermined by, and is a vectorial result of various needs and forces.

The nature and quality of the needs undergo modification as the organism matures and develops. For one thing, these modifications result from transient dominance of given needs—for example, oral over anal, and being fed over feeding oneself—and, consequently, of behavioral modes, with simultaneous recessions of need-behavior modes that were earlier dominant (Erikson, 1959). This results from the inevitable and desirable differentiation of the psychic organization. We have suggested that needs differentiate as the organism develops, and they do so, to some extent, independently of the other co-ordinate of dependence—dependence on the object.

But within the bounds of their individual constitutional anlage and maturational timetable, needs are significantly determined in their characteristics and transformations by the child's early experiences with gratifications. Hartmann, Kris, and Loewenstein (1946) have drawn attention to the important concept that an optimal balance must exist between gratification and frustration for sound development of the psychic organization.

Let us look at the needs more closely.

1. *Physiological needs*

Needs for food and sleep are cyclic, perpetual and imperative for life. The needs for food modify: from milk to solids; so do needs for sleep: from 18-20 hours a day to seven to eight hours a day or less in the adult. Such needs do not obtain the same degree of differentiation as the libidinal and ego-developmental needs.

2. *Libidinal needs*

The libidinal needs, especially the affectional ones, are vastly more complex than the physiological.

A. *Sensual* needs are not manifestly rhythmic in man as they are in some animals, although Benedek and Rubenstein (1942) have shown cyclic affective and behavioral changes in women which correlated with the hormonal rhythm of the menstrual cycle. The basis of the sensual needs is organic; but, as Freud (1905) has described, these take on a psychologic meaning and an autonomy which have great motivational force, perhaps totally determining man's behavior vis-à-vis his sensual needs and his patterns of gratification. A considerable portion of psychoanalytic literature deals with this profoundly important aspect of man's life and its determinants in his psychic development.

B. *Affectional* needs are at the core of the emotional dependence and their gratification is imperative for normal psychic development. Foremost in this category are the needs for affectional love. We do not mean here the "whole sexual current" of the libido as defined by Freud in 1915 (see Chapter 1). Rather we use the term to denote here the libidinal supplies referred to by Spitz (1945a, 1946b, etc.) Mahler (1952 on), Ribble (1943), and others, that is, the currency of "emotional refueling" so aptly described by Pine and Furer (1963).

Affectional love from the object insures not only emotional support and all the activities required of the object by the child's ego-developmental needs, but also his protection and care.[1] The importance of these affectional needs has been discussed by Spitz (1945 on), Mahler (1952 on), Ribble (1943), and others. Spitz (1946) for example, has given us the term anaclitic depression to describe the clinical syndrome in the infant who from about six to 12 months, at the onset and height of psychological dependence, loses the newly-formed libidinal object for an extended period of time.

These affectional needs are not cyclic, in a biological sense. Rather they are based on *psychological balances* determined by the complemental status of intrapsychic and extrapsychic conditions. Epigenetically throughout development, the intrapsychic balance greatly determines what is needed from the extrapsychic component. The balance also determines affects and motivation with reference to these needs. Depression[2] and anger for example, are often the manifestations of a negative balance in libidinal economy. The model of homeostasis is useful. A certain range of equilibria within the psychic organization, as well as between intrapsychic and extrapsychic life, is tolerable, and

---

[1] The categorization of the needs for protection and care is problematic. As auxiliary-ego functions they could fall, logically enough, into the ego-developmental category. However, although these needs do not arise from the instinctual drives as do those for affectional love and sensual gratification, the gratification provided by protection and care contributes significantly to the progressive forging of the object cathexis and the stabilization of the libidinal object. It is on this basis that we have grouped needs for protection and care under the libidinal category.

[2] As Freud (1926) proposed with respect to signal anxiety, some affects are also in the service of the ego to effect adaptive maneuvers. Thus, Saul (1951) and Bibring (1953), as well as Engel (1962), Engel and Reichsman, (1956), and Zetzel (1965) have suggested that depression too, may have an adaptive function. Of course, hostile-aggressive behavior is often used by children and adult humans, and perhaps by animals to signal intent to fight, to hold onto possessions.

adaptive maneuvers occur to maintain an optimal equilibrium.

Libidinal equilibrium and well-being are determined by the interplay of the status and level of development of the psychic organization (with resultant inner sustainment [see Chapter 3]), the individual's relation to objects (sustainment from without), and the dynamic stresses imposed by particular life events.

The level of development and the *status of the psychic organization*, at a given point in time for the particular human being, are critical factors in determining how much each variable contributing to the equilibrium may provide. Thus, very early in psychologic life, the parents (external source) contribute much if not all of the love needed; whereas from latency on, much of the love that sustains the individual comes from his superego (intrapsychic source). A. Freud (1962, 1963) has pointed to the important concept of *age-adequate function and behavior* as well as to the evolving and the differentiation of the psychic organization in the concept of *lines of development.*

The interplay of internal and external sources of libidinal support, as determined by the level of development of the psychic organization, is readily seen in early development as, for example, in the phenomenon of "emotional refueling" described by Pine and Furer (1963). The 15-month-old may be ambulating from one activity to another, quite separate from his mother, but he will from time to time cast a glance at her or briefly approach her to refuel emotionally and then return to his separateness. We would extend in time this concept, proposing that, in a broadened sense, emotional refueling is a process that is ongoing in the human being from the beginning (ego differentiation) to the end of psychologic life, fluctuating in intensity depending on the dynamics that determine his inner sustainment.

The individual's relation to objects is the principal source of support from without (see Chapter 3). We have emphasized the perpetual need for the object, a need which waxes and wanes throughout life. Its importance in early life has been demonstrated by Spitz's (1946b) observation of anaclitic depression in infants. He found that the infants who became anaclitically depressed were those who were forming a "sufficient" libidinal relationship with the mother. Those who were not forming such a libidinal relation did not become depressed when the object was lost. Furthermore, it is our impression that many mature adults are unaware of their needs for affectional love and support, so long as they have a love object who gratifies these. But none who has cathected an object sufficiently escapes recognition of this fact eventually, for object loss leads to mourning. There is little doubt that, in normal as well as pathological mourning, the loss of the anaclitic object, in both children and adults, is a large determinant of mourning.

We have suggested that specific life events which have a stress effect for a given individual inflict a shift in his well-being. Certain current external and internal events, because of genetic and dynamic factors, have stress-specificity (Saul and Lyons, 1952), i.e., they are attached to some past, now more or less unconscious, trauma. Such stress will tax the psychic equilibrium and will lead to a responsive affective, and then adaptive, reaction. Stress will not only lead to dynamic shifts in the psychic organization but will also effect shifts in the economy of the libido.

Briefly then, these three factors determine the need for love (libidinal nutriment) and they operate dynamically, interdependently: the more mature the psychic organization, the more stable and available good object relations, the less stress-specific life events, the less the dependent libidinal needs. It would seem, then, that (in man) there is no biological rhythmicity nor is there a psychological rhythmicity to the need for love.

3. *Ego-Developmental needs*

This side of the child's dependence we would propose to be the essentially *non-libidinal* aspect of dependence on the parents. A dichotomy of *libidinal* and *non-libidinal* needs may well disintegrate under closer scrutiny. It is a most problematical issue, which arises out of the necessity to include in our examination of the child's dependence those aspects of ego functioning which come from sources other than instinctual drives.

We have in mind the help parents provide in the development of functions of the ego, the organ of adaptation (Hartmann, 1939), in contrast to the parents' role in the gratification of drive-derived needs (id cathexes). This non-libidinal dependence arises *vis-à-vis* the development of: (1) inherent biologic activity as primary autonomous ego functions which form the nuclei for cognitive development; and, (2) self-preservative functions, skills for survival in society, which remind us of Freud's self-preservative instincts of pre-1914.

Where we speak of libidinal affectional needs, we refer to the need for emotional refueling for emotional support, protection and care; in the last two, as we noted earlier, the distinction between libidinal and nonlibidinal becomes unclear to us.

We refer to needs as being nonlibidinal if their existence does not arise from the instinctual drives per se (as we now understand the drives). That such needs may become invested with libido and aggression is well known; for example, the child seeks approval for learning to find a hidden ball because he has previously pleased his parents when he has found it. In this sense, searching for a hidden object does not have a primary libidinal component, but obtains one secondarily. Of course, that secondary libidinal component is often a powerful activator of autonomous ego developmental activity; and indeed, there are times when such searching, exploratory activity is determined *primarily* by an id cathexis, i. e., for the prime purpose of getting love.

The in-essence nonlibidinal dependence emerges in relation to those activities of the ego having to do with the development of skills for adaptation. The child depends on his parents for acquiring skills which, in general, range from the development of motor coordination and muscular control, through the development of attention, memory, perception, and cognition; to communication (speech, reading, writing, etc.); which range also from the development of inherent potential in all aspects of intellectual functioning including concept formation and problem solving, to some aspects of play and fantasy, and to skills for work. The child is dependent for learning to do for himself things which were earlier done for him—to feed himself, tie his shoes, handle tools, make decisions, and the like.

We believe that the whole area of cognitive development as investigated and formulated by Piaget, falls into this area of autonomous ego development. We underline here that the child relies on the object to provide an environment optimally enriched with stimuli, opportunities, and accommodations complemental to his maturational schedules. Our experiences with children of deprived environments have confirmed this.

It should be quite clear that, in our view, *libidinal and ego-developmental needs do not emerge in isolation one from the other*; on the contrary, *they emerge hand in*

hand, influence each other and make their claims equally.
We have seen, and others (Mahler, 1963, 1965; Spitz,
1946b, 1965) confirm the presence of significant ego defects in areas of autonomous ego functions as well as in
object relations, defenses, synthetic function and, control
of instinctual drives, in children brought up under conditions of "significant enough" libidinal deprivation. (See
also Piaget [1954, 1962] who proposes that development
of cognitive and affective [i. e., emotional] structures occurs simultaneously.)

Mastery

As every observer knows, within the first year of life we
see remarkable attempts at adaptation to the environment,
both internal and external: sitting, walking, remembering,
recognition, socialization, including communication, and
the development of affects. We have all seen the remarkable efforts *the child makes* at self-education, at mastery,
at engaging his parents and other interested objects when
help is needed (Mahler, 1963, 1965). We also want to
underline here: we do not ignore that doing things without
help, independently, is hardly foreign to the child. Without
the myriad attempts to do things himself, the child would
obtain no degree of autonomy in skills. The periods of
practice that ensure reliable performance and skills are often periods of independent action. But we focus here on
his dependence in attaining optimal ego development.

Note, however, that although we are emphasizing dependent aspects of ego development, we are of course by
no means suggesting passivity. In obtaining the help he
needs, the individual is invariably quite active: the baby
cries, or he screams for help; the toddler takes his mother

by the hand and insistently pulls her to get the toy he wants; the student asks the teacher how to do the project or solve a problem; the adolescent asks her friend how she acts on a date; the parents ask the pediatrician or teacher how to handle a given situation with their child.

Stabilization in the development of ego functions and skills is most important to the whole process of adaptation. Ego development proceeds from the mastery of one ego task[3] after another, from the first steps taken by the primary autonomous ego apparatuses, to the decision-making of the legislator, the lawyer, the physician, or the parent. The need for mastery, seen in relation to ego tasks, is particularly prominent in the anal phase of psychosexual development, for which Peller (1965)·suggested the name: the mastery phase. However, it is our impression, that mastery, as considered by Fenichel (1945), Erikson (1959) and especially Hendrick (1942), is a more ubiquitous factor in the development from childhood to adulthood than suggested by Peller. We believe that one sees a peak of such activity not only in the anal phase but also in the adolescent phase. A. Freud (1936) observed that in adolescence a prominent danger comes from the increased pressure of instinctual drives. At this time the ego's activities in relation to these drives consist in large part of a process of mastery by activity that is adaptive (including defense activity) and accompanied by rechanneling—disengagement and re-investment—of cathexes. It is, perhaps, of some significance that, as Mahler (1963, p. 322) observes, both the anal and adolescent phases exhibit a great degree of activity in the service of separation-individuation and in reorganization of the psychic apparatus.

[3]We do not mean here the great phase-specific ego tasks defined by Erikson (1959) with reference to the development of ego identity. Rather, we mean the myriad activities of the ego, such as the child's learning to tie his shoes, write his name, make decisions, etc.

It seems that the term "mastery" warrants a broader context, beyond activity characteristic of a given phase. In his early writings, Freud suggested that mastery was a part-instinct of the self-preservative type. Fenichel (1945) states that "Mastery means the ability to handle outer and inner drives, to postpone gratification when necessary, to assure satisfaction even against hindrances; it is a general aim of every organism but not of a specific instinct" (p. 13). We see it as a major force, an activity dictated by the self-preservative instincts, impelling the ego to develop a capability that ensures adaptation. And we emphasize the sequential interrelation of: *helplessness of the ego* (state of the ego), *anxiety* (affect experienced by the ego), *mastery* (activity of the ego) *and adaptation* (function of the ego).

We see then, within the first year, adaptational activity that is motivated from within the child, which on the one hand has an autonomous origin, but, on the other hand, depends for success largely on the objects in the environment. During the first year the child *demands*, on the basis of infantile narcissism and omnipotence, and *learns*, in an "average expectable environment" (Hartmann, 1939), that he can get help from his parents. The need for this help, however, arises not only from infantile narcissism (demands and expectations) but equally from the maturational push of inherent activities of the psychic apparatus.[4]

The child's earliest efforts then are heavily dependent on the object for success; indeed, under satisfactory conditions the object optimally encourages such attempts and insures success. Without the functions of the object as teacher and model, each human were he able to survive, would have to start life without the benefit of the experi-

[4]It is not clear to us whether there is a relation of the aggressive drive to this maturational push.

ences of those who have preceded him, at the beginning of civilization.

At the outset, the mother's activity is maximal. But as the ego develops, the assumption of responsibility falls more and more to the child. Yet, while the child develops increasingly complex skills and greater self-reliance, he continues to require the help of others. Midway in childhood, teachers and school take up the process of training in specific areas of development. To be sure, the high value man has placed on increasingly complex education has notably prolonged a young person's dependence.

The development of ego skills, man's tools for effecting adaptation, are greatly enhanced and accelerated by the help provided by the parents, teachers, and society. Again, the pattern for getting help is one that emerges from the earliest period of dependence. Eventually, self-reliance includes knowing how and where to get help when it is required.

DEPENDENCE ON SUBSTITUTES FOR THE OBJECT

Dependence on substitutes for the object is a permutation of dependence on the libidinal object. Winnicott (1953) introduced us to this in his concept of the "transitional object." We see it in part as an anthropomorphizing of the inanimate object—by displacement of object cathexes upon it. The inanimate object is a substitute for the animate object and has attributed to it certain functions or is the recipient of certain affects for which the animate object is made unavailable.

This phenomenon is seen as well in the cathexis of a house as a symbol of parents and family life. In one clinic known to us, patients discharged from a psychiatric ward in the general hospital are seen in the clinic where the resident staff rotates; the patients thus usually do not see the same doctor from one visit to the next. Consequently "the clinic" has come to represent the source of help rather than the person of the doctor. Patients refer to "good" hospitals and "bad" hospitals, depending, among other factors, on the qualities of service they receive.

Reider (1953) observes that "it is now commonplace knowledge that an institution serves many patients as a haven of refuge, wherein they feel more secure and experience . . . protection" (p. 58). Referring to an outpatient psychiatric clinic similar to that described above, he notes that the patients would usually say, "I have an appointment at the clinic," rather than "I have an appointment with Dr. X" (p. 59). Reider observes that some patients will come to the clinic and sit in the waiting room even when their therapist is on vacation.

Reider also remarks, in a comparative reference to the church and the minister, that for some,

> it is the institution which has meaning for them, and the minister is simply the agent of the church who exists for them primarily as an impersonal representative of a mightier power. So it is with clinics and hospitals. As soon as a medical institution achieves a reputation it is a sign that an idealization and condensation of the magical power and the benevolent greatness of parental figures have been positive in the institution. . . . This phenomenon is widespread and it touches upon every type of institution which has any characteristic of benevolence [p. 60].

Weech (1966) notes that some narcotic addicts refer to their home, friends, and acquaintances as "the street". Weech observes that the term seems to have "a multitude of meanings." Thus, the meaning culled out from the associations to the term lead one to assume that the refer-

ence implies, mother, family members, peers, neighborhood, etc. Weech notes the substitutive nature of the concept "the street" by pointing out that the move of the
family out into "the street" is hardly the product of the
satisfactory evolving of separation-individuation. He
writes: "The 'turning to the street' is not the product of
maturation and a gradual independence from primary ties,
but rather the product of a flight into an area which beck-
ons with the promise . . . of infantile gratifications" (1966,
p. 304).

School comes to represent a total system on which
the child depends for development of specific skills.
Home is such a phenomenon too. Of itself it is symbol-
ically complex, but refers principally to shelter, drive
gratifications, and object relations. Work, hospital,
church, the community, the country are such inanimate
(if you will) systems to which humans turn for "care,
love and protection."

There is little doubt that in these transformations of
dependence on objects to dependence on inanimate constructs, a displacement and modifications of object cathexes occur. Whatever the reasons for this permutation
of dependence, it may be of interest to note the nature of
the earliest (narcissistic) object cathexes. According to A.
Freud (1947, 1954) and Spitz (1965b), the cathexis of the
object in earliest infancy is preceded by the cathexis of the
experience gestalt in which the object participates and
from which the object is later differentiated.

We do not propose that cathexis of an institution is
always or even usually regressive. On the contrary, it is
often desirable and is an advance for both the individual
and society. Undue dependence on institutions, however,
may well be regressive; a defense erected in substitution
for object relations. Here, substitution for the object,

where the sufficiently cathected object now fails the subject, probably partakes of two factors: a degree of de-differentiation to a relatively undifferentiated gratification gestalt in which the object loses its focussed cathectic valence; and displacement of archaic parental representations onto an ideological construct as occurs in the transitional object and in the formation of religious ideas.

SUMMARY

Dependence has two co-ordinates: dependence on the object, and dependence for the gratification of needs. Each co-ordinate differentiates epigenetically. Each influences the other in that certain objects arouse specific id cathexes which are experienced as more or less specific need-configurations, and certain needs arouse a search for an object with more or less specific gratification characteristics.

The degree to which the individual is incapable of bringing about gratification of needs by his own action, determines the degree to which he is dependent on the object. The characteristics of this co-ordinate are determined by the development of ego autonomy and competence, by shifts in object cathexes under the impetus of psychosexual development, and by the degree of inner sustainment.

Two factors must be borne in mind in terms of the object *vis-à-vis* the needs: The helplessness of the human neonate makes it utterly dependent on the object; and certain needs, by their nature, and under the aegis of Eros, require the object for gratification, i. e., they are *nonautoerotic*.

The second co-ordinate, dependence for the gratification of needs, is the *raison d'être* of dependence. We have emphasized that the three broad categories of needs: physiological; libidinal,—both sensual and affectional; and ego-developmental, have no clear boundaries; that they influence each other and indeed, need-configurations often partake of more than one category. Needs undergo modification as the organism matures and develops. The characteristics of libidinal needs are determined in part by the status and level of development, by the balance between inner sustainment and the character of object relations (sustainment from without), and by the presence of stress-specific events.

We have proposed that there are nonlibidinal needs for which the parental environment is essential. In this context, primary autonomous ego apparatuses that subserve cognition and certain self-preservative aspects of ego functioning are often not activated by id-cathexes but by nonlibidinal adaptational activity. Much of cognitive development comes under this aspect of ego development. In what may appear to the reader as a historical regression, one can see in this suggestion Freud's pre-1914 formulation of the dichotomy: self-preservative (ego) instincts and libidinal (sexual) instincts. We find this a complex problem. We underline that if such a dichotomy exists, libidinal and ego-developmental needs emerge complementarily and are thus subject to the principle of multiple function.

In the development of the psychic organization, and particularly of ego functions, mastery is a central activity of the ego which ensures the development of skills for adaptation. In this sense, mastery is an inherent characteristic of the ego, activated by both the pleasure and reality principles.

We have also noted that dependence on the object, by dedifferentiation and/or displacement of object cathexes, becomes substituted for by dependence on an inanimate psychic representation such as institutions, hospitals, or "the nation"; this happens also in the transitional object and in religious ideas. This substitution occurs both in normal and in pathological forms.

5. An Epigenesis
of Psychologic Dependence

In an effort to show both the quantitative and qualitative differences between dependence in the child and in the adult, we now trace epigenetically[1], on the basis of the data and formulations we have considered in the previous chapters, the differentiating steps in both co-ordinates of dependence. We preface our examination of the status of differentiation of the needs and object relations for each period with a comment on the epigenetic issues relevant for that period. In considering the first three years of life,

[1] The epigenetic principle has proven useful for concepts of psychic development. It is central to Anna Freud's (1963) "lines of development" and to Mahler's (1965) formulations of self-object differentiation from normal autism through separation-individuation. Erikson, who introduced the principle to psychoanalysis (1950), has applied it to psychosexual differentiation (1950) and to the development of the ego and of the personality (1959). Erikson (1959) defines it thus: "Somewhat generalized, this principle states that anything that grows has a *ground plan*, and that out of this ground plan the *parts* arise, each part having its *time* of special ascendency, until all parts have arisen to form a *functioning whole*" (p. 52). (For a more extensive discussion of this principle see Erikson (1950, pp. 65-67.)

we have adhered to Mahler's (1965, 1967, 1968b) phases and subphases of self-object differentiation.

BIRTH TO FOUR MONTHS

Epigenetic Issues:

During the normal autistic phase, the neonate is utterly helpless, its dependence grossly biological. Need gratification is mediated from the side of the neonate by biophysiological mechanisms: homeostatic, instinctive-reflexive, primary autonomous ego function. As libido differentiates (Jacobson, 1964; Spitz, 1953, 1965), gratification experiences become transiently libidinized for longer and longer periods. The ego task is to recognize that help comes from without (Mahler, 1952). The id-ego begins to differentiate during the period from six weeks to three months of age. Mahler's concept suggests that primary autonomous ego functioning must operate sufficiently for the infant to recognize by three to four months that help comes from without.

The Needs:

We do not think it necessary, for our current purpose, to elaborate on the ever-present, generally cyclical needs for food, fluids, sleep, and the like. Although we know that physiologic needs may be subject to erotization and may be used as substitutes for psychic gratification of dependent love needs, sex, or for release of or dealing with aggression, we shall content ourselves with mentioning them here and concentrate solely on the libidinal and ego-developmental needs.

Libidinal–affectional: Although not perceived psychically (diacritically–Spitz, 1965b) by the organism, many
psychoanalytic investigators (Spitz, 1946 on; Mahler, 1952
on; Benedek, 1949; Ribble, 1943; Balint, 1953; and
others) believe that libidinal need gratification, "maternal
love," is required for normal development as "psychic
nutriment." As the attachment to a cloth which Harlow's
monkeys demonstrated, such needs can be present at or
near birth in some precocial species where they are mediated directly by IRM-reflex mechanisms. The human neonate does not "demonstrate" these needs until ego functioning develops further.

Libidinal–sensual: Sucking (IRM-based) is the proto-
typical sensual activity for this period. Most infants very
soon become capable of some autoerotic gratification in
this mode. We assume that sensual gratification may reside
in proprioceptive, labyrinthine, and skin-contact apparatuses through which perception begins (Spitz, 1965). At
the outset, infants require an object as, for example, in
rocking and being held. Some autoerotic gratification is
possible, however, and represents the first biologic attempts at mastery.

Ego-developmental: Primary autonomous ego functions
(attention, perception, memory, motor) emerge, and mastery of these begins. The mother facilitates mastery in
feeding, by ensuring an optimal complementation to hunger, of breast or bottle presentation and satisfactory juxta-
position of infant's mouth to the breast or bottle. In addition, stimulation by the mother is essential: she is the
"releaser" (in Lorenz's sense) of many instinctive-learning
interlockings that underlie primary autonomous ego functioning. Feeding, bathing, diapering, rocking, cuddling,

talking, etc., provide such stimulation of primary autonomous ego activity.

The Objects:

The child from birth to four months is utterly dependent on the object for survival. However, we assume that
the libidinal object does not exist (objectless stage of
Spitz, 1965b) for the neonate whose CNS immaturity does
not allow for sufficient differentiation of cognitive functioning or instinctual drives (Jacobson, 1964, Spitz,
1965b) to effect such psychic and libidinal recognition.
Gradually, with cognitive and drive differentiation and
with conditioning, certain experience gestalts become invested with libido, particularly during feeding and crying
periods. Out of these, the human face becomes invested
with differentiating, infantile, narcissistic libido; it evokes
the smiling response between six weeks and three months
of age (Spitz, 1946a, 1965b). Although we do not yet have
a "libidinal object," with the smiling response there is a
responsiveness to (probably IRM-based) and a primitive
recognition of a nonspecific, nonlibidinal object.

Spitz (1946 on) and Mahler (1952 on), as well as Jacobson, (1954, 1964), Ribble, (1943), Balint, (1953) and
Benedek, (1949), have commented on the importance of
the libidinal object. Mahler (1965) states,

> One of the cardinal hypotheses at the base of our research is that
> ... (autonomous) ego functions ... which, according to Hart-
> mann (1939, 1952) are essential for the development of ego au-
> tonomy and belong to the conflict-free sphere of the ego, *need
> the libidinal availability of the mother* for their optimal unfolding
> and synthesis [p. 163, italics added] .

THREE TO SIX MONTHS

Epigenetic Issues:

During the early part of the normal symbiotic phase, the three- to six-month-old is vastly more mature than was the neonate. Its signals have become sufficiently differentiated so that the mother can distinguish between gastric distention or pain from an open pin. Development of primary autonomous ego function and motor function results in an infant who looks alert, sits with support, and holds up its head. Ego functioning is manifest in the stare-with-interest at the stranger, the smile at the face. Some preference (in certain four-month-olds) for the mother is apparent in frequency of smiles for the mother and some whimpering when she leaves the room. We have seen a "stranger response" as early as four and a half months. As cognitive and memory functions increase in capability, the earliest cathexes of experiences occur. With this, the percept of the object begins to differentiate and the earliest cathexes of the face take place. The face-smile sequence stabilizes. Experience stabilizes that most important first step to healthy psychic development, the apperception that help comes from the outside (Mahler, 1952).

The Needs:

Libidinal–affectional: The need for libidinal nutriment is conspicuous. The infant's crying is easily stopped just by the object's picking him up. With hunger satiated, he will sit on a lap with comfort, only to fuss when put in the crib. This fussing may continue for a number of minutes.

We can begin to see now that some libidinal needs are strictly anaclitic: they require the object for their gratification.

Libidinal—sensual: The need to suck may be observed after satisfactory feeding. Some infants suck their thumb after feeding, some with such vigor and persistence that the entire fist seems to be subjected to this exercise. Proprioceptive, skin-contact gratification, even through clothes, assuages crying. Some autoerotic gratification is possible, particularly in sucking. The principal satisfaction of proprioceptive and skin-contact needs requires the object at this age. Autoerotic rocking occurs from the latter part of the first year on.

Ego-developmental: Primary autonomous functions are stimulated and exercised by the object's ministrations. Communication is an extremely important function for which the object is essential. The gradient of frustration-gratification suggested by Hartmann, Kris, and Loewenstein (1946) as essential for optimal psychic development, also requires the object. The four-month-old who wants to be held longer and cries when put into the crib learns that he cannot be continually gratified by being held, that there is a reasonable limit to what he can "get" (Saul, 1947). He receives his first lessons in exercising frustration tolerance, experiencing control of instinctual drives (particularly aggression), in awareness of the importance of the object and in the development of communication with the object, in reality testing, and perhaps in beginning synthetic (integrative) functioning.

The Objects:

The once-a-week babysitter may be as successful as the mother in comforting, feeding, and talking to the two-

month-old infant. Gradually, as early as four months, differentiating between the mother's face and that of others
begins. For example: A four-month-old girl, when visited
by a stranger-observer at whom she had smiled easily and
readily the month before, now studied his face and, after
an unexpectedly protracted delay of about three minutes,
smiled at him. There was no such reserve in smiling at her
mother or sister, nor we are told, at her father. The
"studying" look represented, we believe, early manifestations of the stranger response aroused by increasing capability to perceive that the stranger's face is not one that
often appears in her *Umwelt* and is associated with need
gratification, i. e., the mother. It is interesting that her
three-year-old sister was also guaranteed a smile, although
she did much less than mother to gratify needs. But the
sister by identification with her mother, became an auxiliary care-taker, presenting herself to the crying baby in a
manner quite imitative of her mother. The infant then had
begun the process which eventuated in clearly-expressed
stranger anxiety, as occurred at our next visit. This time
the "studying" period was followed, not by a smile, but by
crying and anxiety. Now the knowledge that help comes
from without is beginning to attach to that percept which
seems to be invariably associated with need gratification—
the mother's face. Differentiation of ego functioning
makes possible the discrimination of gestalts—face, voice,
touch, etc.; beginning differentiation of affects makes possible early "soft" experiences of anxiety; and progressive
cathexes of recognitive representations of the mother's
face—and those of other family members—with libido are
taking place.

SIX TO TEN MONTHS

Epigenetic Issues:

The first subphase of the separation-individuation process, *differentiation*, coincides with that of the differentiation of the object as libidinal object. The child's biologic
dependence—the experiences of need-gratification—has
become libidinized and, conjointly, the dependence has
become psychological. This expresses itself in the experience of anxiety, and is created principally by the ego's
sense of helplessness, brought on by its awareness of the
absence of the libidinal object (Freud, 1926). Separation
anxiety and stranger responses reach a peak. As Spitz and
Wolf have shown (1946b), protracted and nonsubstituted
loss of the libidinal object at this time may lead to anaclitic depression. Mahler (1952; Mahler and Gosliner,
1955) has cited some of the more severe consequences of
arrested or problematic differentiation of self and nonself
in the process of symbiotic childhood psychosis. This subphase of separation—individuation coincides with the latter
part of the normal symbiotic phase during which the infant must recognize the libidinal object as separate from
himself. Recognition of the object as external occurs in
conjunction with progressive internalizations (Hartmann
and Loewenstein, 1962) of the psychic object representation, a process essential to separation-individuation
(Parens, 1970a). Freud held from 1926 on that fear of
loss of the object is the first psychically perceived danger
situation.

With respect to Bowlby's (1958) theory of Component
Instinctual Responses referent to the nature of the human
child's tie to his mother, we point out that clinging, as a
dominant mode in attaching to the object emerges in response to separation anxiety. If clinging has an IRM component, as it seems to have in Harlow's monkeys, the response in man is activated by separation anxiety. It would
appear that in the human child, object-clinging of the type
observed during the differentiation subphase (which is the
first functionally-effective object-clinging seen in the human child) is the product of IRM-learning interlocking.

The Needs:

Libidinal—affectional: Demands for the presence and
ministrations of the libidinal object become intensified.
This results largely from the recognition that the object is
separate from the self, i. e., from the infant ego's experience of helplessness in the absence of its auxiliary ego.
Needs for protection against internal and external danger
are manifest. The most common external dangers are separation from the object and the appearance of the stranger.
Needs for libidinal nutriment also appear in response to
events ranging from normal regression of the ego at bed-
time to unyielding wishes for symbiotic fusion with the
object. Needs for libidinal nutrition become more evident
with greater degree of reciprocal communication between
mother and child. Spitz described (1946b) how, in those
child-mother relations which were good, a more intense
loss reaction occurred upon separation, leading us to de-
duce that a greater degree of object cathexis and libidinal
dependence had developed.

Libidinal–sensual: The dominance of erotogenic excitation continues to reside in the oral cavity. Two principal factors at this time extend the activity of the oral cavity: the continuing maturation and development of the motor apparatus leads to a marked increase in hand to mouth co-ordination, exploration and gratification of excitation (Hoffer, 1949); and the emergence of teeth intensifies even further the cathexis of the mouth with new experiences of pain, solid food, etc. In some children, experiential factors intensify anal and/or phallic excitations which press for gratification with resultant autoerotic manipulation.

With the appearance of separation anxiety and much clinging, contactual stimulation may emerge as a dominant source of need and gratification. Some children violently resist being put down by their mothers at this time; the degree to which anxiety or contact-hunger is responsible may be difficult to assess. Some mothers feel caught between protecting the infant against anxiety and feeling that the little rascal just wants to be held incessantly. Complicated mother and/or child factors generally overdetermine such issues.

Ego-developmental: With the mother's recognition of developing ego functioning, with her knowledge that communication with her infant is in many ways apperceived and reciprocated, and with the appearance of separation anxiety, socialization of the infant gathers momentum. The infant is helped to sit, to crawl, to hold things; the optimal environment facilitates experience, stimulates efforts in development, protects mastery. It also allows and assists in the development of frustration tolerance. (We have seen significant lags in these developments in libidinally deprived children.)

The Objects:

With sufficient differentiation of ego function, the infant recognizes the role of the object in gratifying needs. With this recognition, the psychological dependence becomes object-specific. It is the "specific" object, the mother—or "specific" substitutes such as father—that guarantees gratification. Loss of the object leads to anxiety, then grief and, if seriously protracted and not substituted for, to anaclitic depression. In 1965, Mahler pointed to the importance of this psychologic dependence, observing:

> According to our hypothesis, the core deficiency in infantile psychoses is the infant's and toddler's inability to utilize the symbiotic (need-satisfying) object, 'the external ego' (of the mother) as an outside organizer, to serve his rudimentary ego in the process of orienting and adapting himself to reality [pp. 161-2].

TEN TO FIFTEEN MONTHS

Epigenetic Issues:

During the second subphase of separation-individuation, the *practicing* subphase, most children begin to walk, although the normal range tends to be somewhat wider: nine to 18 months. With locomotor maturation and capacity to use that apparatus, many new issues arise. Now the infant moves away from the object more frequently and for longer periods. Yet separation anxiety still commonly appears when the mother leaves the child. We have already seen from the prior *differentiation* subphase the beginnings of the affectional current of the libido and, we believe, also the beginnings of object libido; these beginnings are significantly advanced during the *practicing* subphase. Valuation of a show of love from the object appears.

The Needs:

Libidinal—affectional: A perceptible change takes place in the infant, a change denoting a quest for libidinal supplies. Toni, a 13-month-old sitting beside her father, clearly responds to two observers who applaud her. Her father asks her to imitate the "Indian call" (open-mouthed falsetto vocal sound, hand to and fro in front of mouth to emit alternately mute and clear sounds.) Toni obliges, then she claps her hands and grins widely. She repeats this and carries out several other performances; each time she looks at the observers, at her father and smiles broadly. Visible are the one-year-old's efforts to obtain approval and her absorption of the object's affectional response, received as an aliquot of libidinal supply. There is also the pleasure of mastering motor coordination as she performs. Parental approval supports efforts at mastery and is indeed a vital force in efforts at mastery; it will play its part in scholastic and other achievements throughout life.

Pine and Furer (1963), as also noted by Mahler (1963), have described this type of phenomenon at this sub-phase of separation-individuation in what they call "emotional refueling." The toddler who has newly found that motor co-ordination and activation takes him away from the object, now and then during his expeditions, returns to the object by a glance or a physical contact that may be quite brief, to then return again to his exploration. The momentary contact, visual or physical, which we have seen so many times, is very aptly described as "emotional refueling."

What Ribble (1943), Spitz, Mahler and others have indicated that the neonate needs now is *sought* by the infant-toddler: libidinal supplies. As Mahler points out, (1965) the child is by no means inactive in his dependence: "It is quite impressive to observe the extent to which the normal infant-toddler is intent upon extracting, and is usually able to extract, contact supplies and participation from the mother, sometimes against considerable odds" (p. 168). We believe that this represents the affectional current of the libido *required* by the infant. This is the beginning of the need for the love from the object which emerges after, and differentiates out of, the need for the object (Freud 1926, Addendum C). Fear of loss of love from the object has two facets: "The need for love which stems from the need for care, and the need for the love itself, for "libidinal nutriment." With this development, psychologic dependence for libidinal supplies, for "protection, care and indulgence" rises into view; in accordance with epigenetic principles, it will stay with man, in one form or another, for the rest of his days.

Libidinal–sensual: Needs to discharge erotically and aggressively through the oral cavity by sucking and biting continue to dominate psychosexually. Teething adds its weight to this oral dominance. Anaclitic contactual needs seem evident in the clinging associated with separation anxiety; such contactual need seems to present also in the contact of emotional refueling. The essential component of the contact behavior which appears in reaction to a dreaded stimulus—often seen in the human as stranger anxiety—is best described by what Harlow observed in his monkeys. When presented with a fear-producing, strange "thing," a toy for example, the frightened infant monkey will avoid the "thing", approach its cloth object, rub its body against the object, and then approach the frightening "thing," recharged, in a sense, with support and libido. Such contactual behavior contains the possibility for multiple gratifications—affectional, protective, and sensual.

Ego-developmental: When there is evidence of emerging locomotor capacity, parents encourage it; some parents, when they see their child begin to walk expect a concomitant degree of self-feeding and verbalization. Especially with reference to speech, these efforts bear little fruit at this time; however, they do set the stage for attempts the toddler will soon make to speak.

As the id and ego differentiate and develop, processes such as internalization and identification are critical factors in that development. Processes such as identification are anaclitic in nature, i. e., the infant identifies with the mother, the father, and, as did Toni, with siblings. Control of instinctual drive derivatives begins: biting is restricted to certain conditions, throwing certain things is discouraged, explorations have their limits, etc.; in these, parents engender developments in the ego which they assist by repeated efforts.

The Objects:

Toni's father tells us that his 13-month-old daughter no longer screams when mother leaves. Just a month before she cried even in her father's arms; now she does not. She eyes the two observers, moves closer to father, smiles, performs, seems very comfortable, and thoroughly relishes approval. Slowly, she maneuvers her way to the observer who had seen her since birth every two to three weeks; later—in good Spitz fashion, except that *she* approaches the observer—she "backs into" the second observer, who has not seen her for six months. A faint shade of anxiety is observable. Upon our leaving, Toni, in her father's arms, puts out her arms to the first observer, and, after very briefly being held, dashes back to her father's arms. The objects in her world are multiplying. None has the primacy of her mother, but the father is now highly libidinized. There is, in addition, a three-year-old brother, much imitated by Toni, who is also a libidinized object. Even the occasional visiting observer is explored and transiently cathected with libido. Inasmuch as the more frequently-seen observer was selected over the second one, both as the first to be approached and as the only one to get a parting contact, it would be plausible to assume the existence of some psychic representation of him. The infant's object world is expanding as a result of explorations of the environment from a base of security and libidinal nutriment: the libidinized object in this case, the father. Harlow (1962, 1966) lucidly described the process in his infant monkeys whose libidinized object was a cloth assemblage. His monkeys, however, only got out what they put in; not so, the parent-raised infants. (See Spitz's [1965a] comments on the need for *reciprocity* between child and mother.)

In our observations the role the father plays in the infant's life in the earliest months is more diffuse than that of the mother. Generally, during the period of early libidinal-object differentiation, the mother is preferred, i. e., is more active as auxiliary ego; however, the father and siblings, of course, stand in a much closer relation to the child than does the stranger. In general, the father does not elicit a stranger response if he is seen from day to day through the first six or so months of life. With the structuring of libidinal objects, our impressions are that the mother has greater valence as specific object during the period under discussion than does the father. Often, for instance the father has to give over the child to his mother for calming during periods of stress because his ministrations do not fulfill their aim. The father, however, is clearly libidinized, taking precedence over siblings who are with the infant more constantly.

Of course, a number of factors contribute to these gradations of cathexis and effectiveness of auxiliary-ego function. This cathexis-gradient will continue into the second year of life, at which point the lagging cathexis and structuring of the father-representation achieves a sufficient degree of stabilization so that we can see two sufficiently-stable dyads each with its particular functions and characteristics.

14 TO 36 MONTHS

Epigenetic Issues:

During the next two subphases, that of *rapprochement*, from 14 to 22 months, and that of *object-constancy*, from 25 to 36 months, locomotor development continues apace. Mastery of sphincter control is a large task of this period; with it, control of instinctual drives abuts vigorously with the environment. Speech, one of the great psychic organizers (Spitz, 1965b) emerges through the continuous process of imitation and identification. The child's behavior begins to reflect dramatically the internalization of the standards and dictates of the external environment in the form of superego precursors. Ego-identifications seem more prominent as parent-like behavior makes its appearance. Structuralization of psychic object and self-representations underlies such identifications. These also lead to

object constancy, the *sine qua non* of satisfactory separation-individuation and of the ability to be alone (Winnicott, 1965).

The Needs:

Libidinal—affectional: The need for love from the parents becomes the great motivator in learning to control
instinctual drives. It is also a great motivator in learning to
speak and to dress oneself. The struggle between gratification of drives and retaining approval, begun during the oral
(biting) phase, looms around toilet-training and will continue in more complex forms in phase-specific conflicts
during the oedipal period, latency, and adolescence. Aggressive drive derivatives projected onto the environment,
as well as increased reality testing, render important to the
child the perceived need to be protected. Fear of loss of
love from the object—which would deny the child his
rights to protection, care and indulgence—is the dominant
danger-situation for this phase of development.

Libidinal—sensual: Epigenetically, the anal phase of
psychosexual development becomes dominant. Gratification is increasingly autoerotic and gratified less by the object than it was in the oral phase. The need for the object
vis-à-vis the sensual needs is largely in terms of the objects'
auxiliary-ego functions. Not uncommonly, however, the
object also stimulates and effects erotic gratifications.
There is also much muscular (other than sphincter) activity
with proprioceptive gratifications, such as acts associated
with expanding locomotor control—tricycle riding, for example. Play, such as finger-painting, has a large tactile-
erotic as well as an olfactory component.

Ego-developmental: The task of the ego in learning to
control, to begin to sublimate and neutralize instinctual

drives mounts sharply. Peller (1965) has emphasized the importance of mastery at this phase, mastery of sphincter control, of speech development, of further motor coordination. The object is the principle teacher and helper of these various ego strivings.

Fantasy and play, which earlier were solitary and fragmentary, develop. Thus a bright 18-month-old can pretend she pulls out a flower from a book of pictures and ask the observer to smell it. Another 18-month-old pretends she is a baby in a tub. The two-year-old can begin to play with a peer. Much of this development is stimulated and supported by the parents; some is autonomous. Here again we note the vast role the object plays in these developments; the clinician and investigator who observes libidinally-deprived children readily sees thwarted development where the object's auxiliary-ego functions are poor.

The Objects:

The need for the object during this period for the purpose of psychic development cannot be over-estimated. Mahler (1963, 1965) has pointed out that object constancy is fundamental to the process of separation-individuation. It is through the repeated process of internalization of the psychic representations of the objects and the simultaneous libidinization of these psychic representations that they achieve such a degree of stabilization that they hold a cathexis even in the absence of the actual object. These internalized representations of the objects, available to the ego which contains them, lead to modifications in self-representations by identification; in a sense, the ego and self-concepts have a fountain of models for adaptation and identity formation. Thus, the object psychically-internalized makes possible eventual separation from the actual object and the capacity to be alone (as described by Winnicott, 1965).

With greater stabilization of the libidinal object, at about 18 to 24 months some differentiation of parental roles becomes evident—within the framework of the generalization that both parents provide protection, care and indulgence. Of course, each individual brings to his role as parent his own total personality, and the variations in parenting are as infinite as are personalities. But generally, we see caretaking and indulgence taken up by mothers, limit-setting by the fathers. In addition, some fathers bring home an unused supply of parental libido at a time when the mother's parenting energy seems to run low. Identification with father during this period consists not only in wanting-to-be-like the admired, idealized father (Freud, 1921) who protects and earns money, but also in "identification with the aggressor" (A. Freud, 1936), in relation to his function as limit-setter; he thereby contributes to both ego and superego-precursors.

The character of object relations has so far been essentially dyadic. During the next year or so, these object relations will complicate significantly. Often during this period (14 to 36 months) the birth of a sibling creates a triadic conflict. However, the basic nature of the conflict, we suggest, is still dyadic. Sibling rivalry emerges with the appearance of a recognized competitor for the attention and libidinal nutriment from the parents. Thus the sibling is a competitor for the symbiotic dyadic set. The possessiveness of the infant-toddler is predominantly narcissistic and arises directly out of the symbiosis with the mother.

The first triad, then, differs significantly from the triad of the phallic phase: first, in that sensual libido (see Chapter 1) is neither genital nor object-directed; that is, the possessiveness for the love object arises from dependent and narcissistic affectional needs. Second, there is no claim for the love object's genital functions for which the child becomes the rival, as occurs in the Oedipus complex; thus the *sibling* is the competitor in the first triad by intruding into the residual symbiotic dyad, but the *child becomes* the competitor in the phallic triad by becoming the intruder in the marital dyad.

This prephallic sibling rivalry triad, however, creates more problems than is indicated in the literature. It underlies much hostile competitiveness, destructiveness and guilt, feelings of worthlessness and shame, and contributes its heavy share to man's neurotic problems.

We should point out as well that the peer or sibling is also an object with whom play is carried out. We have seen some siblings, particularly older ones, assume the role of protector as well as aggressor, *vis-à-vis* the child of this age group.

THREE TO SIX YEARS

Epigenetic Issues:

At this age the process of separation-individuation will have proceeded to a sufficient degree that separation from the object without untoward anxiety and for extended periods of time, will allow for entry into nursery school and kindergarten.

Leading to the emergence of the phallic-genital phase and the Oedipus complex are both biologic processes and the differentiation of object relations from the dyadic to the triadic model. Biologic processes, in accordance with a maturational timetable, lead to dominance of the phallic mode. This occurs in normal children as well as in those who have not proceeded satisfactorily through separation-individuation, those who have been arrested in psychosexual and psychosocial development. Thus one psychotic five-year-old girl frequently masturbates but has not attained object relations beyond an archaic dyadic character.

In the normal child, the sensual-genital current of the libido emerges and is directed, in both boys and girls, to the object that has received the earliest and greatest affectional cathexis: the prime insurer and gratifier of needs, the mother. It is the new cathexis with now-differentiating, object-directed, genital libido that modifies the mother representation from affectional to sexual love-object (Freud, 1915), which leads to the triadic character of these object relations. Now father is experienced as a rival for the gratification, by mother, of newly-emerging impulses.

In attempting to clarify it, one becomes aware of the complexity of libidinal attachment (libidinal object-choice) versus need for libidinal gratification. The need the child has for love and protection from the object is clear enough; it is more difficult to recognize that a cathexis of the object with genital libido, that is, directing one's genital impulses toward the object, is perceived as a need. Freud (1923) made this point clearly: "We can only suppose that ... object-cathexes proceed from the id, *which feels erotic trends as needs*. The ego ... becomes aware of the object-cathexes, and ... acquiesces in them or ..." represses them (p. 29; italics added). Thus the attachment of nonautoerotic libidinal impulses to an object is experienced by the ego as a need (see Chapter 1). The young man who has attached his sexual impulses to the representation of a particular young lady, experiences a powerful need for gratification. Thus, it is the pleasure principle that dictates the object cathexis to be perceived as a need, i. e., to be gratified by the object.

The Oedipus complex and its resolution, with structuralization of the superego as a separate psychical agency, occur during this period. We repeat here that in considering the origins of the superego, Freud (1923) stated that it arises from two factors: the resolution of the Oedipus complex and the long period of helplessness and dependence of the child.

We see an important trend in the three- to six-year-old, the development of altruism, wherein the subject derives pleasure from ensuring the gratification of the object. This is not a simple matter, for in all altruism there is a narcissistic gratification. Still, the vector "to get" from the object (Saul, 1947), characteristic of the prephallic periods of development, here begins to have a component "to give" to the object, a development of great importance to future object relations and parenthood (Saul, 1947).

The Needs:

Libidinal—affectional: The child continues to have the libidinal needs of early childhood. Freud pointed out the role played by the need to retain the father's love in the resolution of the Oedipus complex. In Chapters IV and VII of *Inhibition, Symptoms and Anxiety*, he notes that little Hans loved and needed his father's love and protection. This was also a major thesis in *Totem and Taboo*. Fear of loss of the object and fear of loss of love from the object, dominant at prior phases of development, still have a large influence in the three- to six-year-old child, particularly the fear of loss of love. It is well known that Freud (from 1924 on) ascribed the resolution of the Oedipus complex in the girl to the fear of loss of love from the object. Later, Waelder (1937) stated that *in addition*, the boy experiences the fear of castration. Fear of loss of love from both mother and father are operative for the boy: from the father, because of rivalry with him; from the mother, because for both realistic and unrealistic reasons she rejects the sensual gifts of her five-year-old son. In addition, many parents threaten the child who masturbates with loss of love or even with castration. Because satisfactory resolution of the Oedipus complex is necessary for the further development of the child, the oedipal love-object must frustrate the sensual needs of the child while gratifying optimally the affectional. We not infrequently see parents who globally reject their children as a defense against their own responsiveness to the child's not always unconscious sensual wishes. This occurs, in some cases, during the oedipal phase, in others, during adolescence.

Libidinal–sensual: We assume in accordance with the theories of biology and the theory of Eros as proposed by Freud from 1920 on that the aim of the genital impulses is the preservation of the species. On the basis of Eros, the genital impulses seek the object and need the object for ultimate gratification; yet for normal development these impulses must be diverted from their infantile goal, the primary love-object. We now have evidence from ethology (particularly Lorenz [1935, 1953], Hess [1959], and others [see Chapter 2], who have described the directing of sensual behavior toward the object of primary attachment) that supports Freud's postulates referent to the directing of genital impulses toward the primary love-object at the time of their first emergence. We suggest, then, that the genital impulses are biologically anaclitic, that they need the object for their target as well as for their source of gratification.

Ego-developmental: Further mastery of locomotor activity and speech is stimulated and supported by the parents. The rapid expansion of skills is facilitated by the adult whose mediation of many activities encourage their development. In this sense, too, use of materials at school, the beginnings of peer-play and learning activities, including help in achieving further degrees of frustration tolerance, etc., are critical skills for present and future functioning. Learning to tolerate separation from home may, at this time, take the combined efforts of child, parent, and teacher. We well know the "school refusals" that come from the mother's inability to tolerate or to help the child tolerate separation. A. Freud (1962, 1963) has called attention to the many skills and capacities that must be developed in order for a child to enter nursery school. Our daily contacts with parents testify to the degree to which parents take such development for granted and underestimate the great amount of work put into it by the child and themselves.

As much as the care-taking adult is needed for these developments, we also see a great deal of activity and development initiated and sustained by the child himself. From this period particularly, the child, with his recently acquired ego autonomy, more and more becomes the principle mediator in his own development. But again we stress that under optimal conditions, the object insures further development in all aspects of ego-functioning (Beres, 1956).

The Objects:

The triadic character of object relations in the phallic-oedipal phase needs little further emphasis here. The need for the object is no less great here than it was before. Indeed, A. Freud (1963) describes this as "the completely object-centered phallic-oedipal phase" (p. 248). The love object is a necessary condition for the emergence of the Oedipus complex. As we mentioned earlier the absence of satisfactory, age-adequate object cathexis, as it appears in some borderline and psychotic children, leads to phallic masturbation but not to an oedipal complex (Rosenfeld and Sprince, 1963).

The role of the parents in the triad of the phallic-oedipal period is complex, has been extensively detailed in psychoanalytic writings, and need not be restated here. The identifications arising from the Oedipus complex and its resolution, bring about differentiations of psychic structure and identity formation of great importance. Again, process in normal development can be highlighted by observations of pathological development. For instance, a four-and-a-half-year-old boy with an unresolving Oedipus complex, indeed a stabilizing negative Oedipus complex (Freud, 1926), likes pink, plays with dolls selectively, is preoccupied with dresses and long hair and walks like a girl; as a witch, in fantasy he wants to marry his father, and ten minutes later, wants to kill him. This precocious (in its degree of consolidation) feminine identification, existing already for over one year, stands as a defense erected against the boy's wishes to displace his father and the consequent dangers this entails.

As this case illustrates, unsuccessful resolution of the Oedipus complex can, of course, obstruct appropriate sexual identity formation. Dominance in identification with the parent (actual or fantasied) of the *same* sex is a prime result of a successfully-resolved Oedipus complex. We will not go into the complexities whereby a boy's *rivalry* with his father *is converted, through an identification,* into altruism and a "giving up" of the oedipal love-object, his mother (i. e., how the child who loses the oedipal love-object substitutively identifies with the oedipal rival-object rather than with the object which is "given up"). (See Chapter 1).

According to Freud (1926), each parent makes a contribution as love object and as rival at this period. Essentially, for the boy, the father continues to serve both as love object (of the pre-phallic period) and protector, and now as competitor for the mother's love. During this period the boy's new wish to displace his father becomes modified to one of being like him, a wish that has an antecedent in the prephallic phase (Freud, 1921). It is our impression that, by the time of the phallic phase, the parents have become objects with equal cathectic valence. However the mother generally becomes phallic love-object before the father, for both boy and girl, not necessarily because she is more libidinized at this time, but because genetically she was cathected first and she first aroused, and often still does, erotogenic impulses (through her ministrations). Without elaborating on the complex issue of the roles the parents play at this period, suffice it to say that each object now has well defined functions whatever these may be in each family, and the child essentially knows them in that cast.

The nursery school and kindergarten youngster may find a peer object, to whom he becomes strongly attached. Two four-year-old girls had selected each other in nursery school and were frequently together; often they fought and as often made-up. The absence of one from school was readily observable in the other child. That a school child who befriends a peer will experience loss-affects when the peer object is absent indicates the ability to cathect the representation of a peer at this period. Certainly, such peer libidinization occurs in siblings prior to this phallic-oedipal phase. We have seen a six-month-old infant whose three-and-a-half-year-old sister could make smile broadly in the presence of two strangers who had unequivocally aroused anxiety. The older sister had received a share of the infant's symbiotic-phase libido which carried a remarkable valence. We have seen other examples of para-mother libidinization at the period of emerging object-specificity, although this case was striking in its consistency and vigor. Neighborhood peers become significant objects as well, during the phallic phase.

LATENCY

Epigenetic Issues:

As Freud (1905, 1923) observed, the latency period of psychosexual development seems to be peculiar to man. We have no indication from the work of Harlow et al. (1959, 1960, 1962, 1966) that such a "diphasic onset of . . . sexual life" (Freud, 1923, p. 35) occurs in monkeys, which pass from infancy to the juvenile and then adolescent stages. In the domesticated dog (Scott, 1963), these sequential stages are even more telescoped and again, so far as we know, no indication of a diphasic onset of sexual life has been described. It is likely that the diphasic phenomenon in man is the product of biologic and psychologic, experiential factors. The passing of the phallic-oedipal phase brings with it the emergence of the superego and the repression and sublimation of phallic-oedipal impulses. To continue our simplified schema: the ego joined by the superego, imposes continued repression and sublimations until these are challenged by the immense upsurge of instinctual drives associated with puberty. This biological upsurge initiates the second onset of sexual life.

The degree to which, in latency, the psychic structure is challenged by pressing instinctual drives should not be underestimated. Efforts to control masturbation and sex play and an interest in sexual matters are readily observable, particularly—but not only—in boys. Many will giggle, suddenly act silly, when the adult answers a question just raised by the youngster himself. On the other hand, they also deal with such drives by reaction formation. Some will ridicule the adult's answer and claim innocence of thought and action. Others will dismiss a question raised by a peer as foolish, stupid. Thus the latency period is a dynamic state in which the multiple function of psychic structure maintains sexual activity and fantasy at a low ebb in comparison with the two peak phases it essentially helps to create, i. e., the oedipal and puberty.

The tasks of the ego during this period continue to be large and constant. Large demands are made of the ego by formal education and the push to 'industry' (Erikson, 1959). Of great significance at this time too is the expansion of the environment and the emerging importance of peer relations. Also relevant are the attachments to adult objects other than parents. It is essentially a period of relative and gradual stabilization of psychic structure, of identity, and of character formation.

The Needs:

Libidinal—affectional: The sources for libidinal supplies as well as for care and protection are still largely the parents. However, there arises from the structuralization of the superego a most significant development which greatly enhances the individual's autonomy. The superego, now an internal agency, can, by the dynamics and economics of libido, approve of, commend, and love the subject. It joins object constancy in importance in securing autonomy of the individuating subject. With emergence of psychic structure now differentiated into its principal agencies, the organism has a psychic organization that can begin a self-reli-

ant social existence, that is, it now has the ability to obtain
by its own actions what it needs for survival, satisfaction,
and successful living. In addition to love from the superego
(the reader will recognize the phase-dominant danger situation: fear of loss of love from the superego), ego-ideal/ego
processes also participate in the economy of libido needed.
We are reminded of Freud's concept of self-esteem (self-
regard) formulated in one brilliant stroke in the paper "On
Narcissism" (1914). Self-esteem has three sources: the first
is primary—the residue of infantile narcissism; the second
is the omnipotence which is corroborated by experience,
the fulfillment of the ego ideal; while the third source is
"the satisfaction of object-libido", i. e., gratification of
anaclitic needs, affectional and sensual (p. 100). Note that
in the second point, the ideal-directed achievements of the
ego are a source of self-service of libido and aid the subject's sustainment from within, what we have called inner
sustainment (see Chapter 3).

Although there is now a considerable degree of autonomy in the economy of the libido, that is, there is a progressively developing source of libidinal supplies from within,
parents are still the principal sources of protection, care,
and indulgence. In addition, now peers begin to play an
important role in that economy, by being a source of mutual companionship, comfort, and commiseration about in-
justices inflicted by parents, teachers, and siblings, as well
as unfriendly peers. Peers are also suppliers of sources 2
and 3 of self-esteem.

Libidinal—sensual: As we noted in describing epigenetic
issues for this period, sensual needs are only relatively qui-
escent. They tend to be dealt with autoerotically, the object being dissimulated in fantasies or detached (repressed)
from the activity. Among siblings and peers, some mutual
genital play is common. Solitary masturbation as the tem-

porary chosen path for the gratification of genital impulses may occur in early or late latency.

Ego-developmental: Development of intelligence and skills, propelled by maturation, is engendered both by the expectations from the environment and, now, from the self through the ego ideal. For this development, the latency youngster leans on the parents—to help with homework, to repair a shelf or a door, on his teachers—for daily instructions, and on peers—to practice catching a ball, the mutual assistance each provides the other.

There is an unequivocal need for these objects for the development of ego functioning, achieved particularly through identification, especially in the control and modulation of instinctual drives, thought processes and communications, reality testing, and successful object relations (Beres, 1956). We also noted above the importance of these objects for the development of autonomous ego functions. In addition, the objects, particularly the parents, are still of great importance to the latency youngster in their auxiliary ego and superego functioning.

The Objects:

During latency, the parents continue to be objects for identification which serves to further consolidate sexual identity in both boys and girls. The father especially is the representative of work, industry (Erikson, 1959) and responsibility.[2] Father is still looked to for protection and limit-setting. Functioning as the external superego, he continues to play a prominent part in intrapsychic and behavior control. He is also a chosen companion for his children

[2] We believe this may have much to do with the misconception even many grown men and women have, that women do little valuable work as mothers and homemakers.

who value his abilities even while rivalry with him exists. This is particularly true for the first phase of latency, usually waning with the second phase, when peers tend to further increase in importance.

Heretofore, object relations, dyadic and triadic, consisted dominantly of the child-parent relations. Although for many children, siblings have already played a significant role as objects prior to latency, the peer as an object now gains in importance as a result of the ongoing process of separation-individuation and the working through of the Oedipus complex. Significant is the repression of impulse derivatives from the phallic-oedipal phase, thereby abetting the cathexis of objects other than the parents. In association with the changes in relations between child and parents and the freeing of object libido, new objects are sought, a process facilitated by separation from parents during school periods and the presence of peers for many hours during that time. Significantly operative as well, is the process observed in (other) animals high in the scale of phylogeny, wherein the young of the species turn to each other for play and for socialization. That this process has IRM-learned interlocking factors is suggested by the fact that it leads to the socialization, the formation of object relations among peers which eventuate in sexual behavior, reproduction, and the preservation of the species. Thus, for example, Scott (1963) observes that *peer* relations in the dog and other canines are secured by the early appearance of these relations which thus guarantee the social structure of the canines, the pack. Harlow noted the significance of peer relations in monkeys (1962, 1966), and described the complex development of play and socialization among the peer group. The peer group in both dog and monkey seems to be the principal arena where sex emerges. Certainly much incest occurs in the animal kingdom; one must observe, however, that generation boundaries, at least among the domesticated dog, seem lost, once maturity is reached.

During the phallic-oedipal period, the emerging genital libido follows the path of the affectional current, already established as a result of early dependence, and is attached to the parents. That genital libido is then, for well-known reasons, disengaged from the primary love object. Although during the latency period, peers become objects of attachment, this attachment does not generally carry with it the genital libido which has been partly repressed, partly sublimated, and against the emergence of which the ego continues to defend. The end result of the ego's various ways of dealing with these libidinal impulses in latency is the development of peer object relations, feebly invested with genital libido, when compared with the phallic-oedipal and puberty phases. Also, during latency, the peer object cannot serve the protective and caring functions of the parental, adult object, and therefore cannot substitute for the adult anaclitic object.

ADOLESCENCE[3]

Epigenetic Issues:

The second onset of sexuality in man, to paraphrase Freud, is precipitated by the upsurge of genital impulses associated with hormonal and bodily changes of puberty. The arousal of residual, former genital cathexes of oedipal

[3]To simplify our task we have not divided the phase of adolescence into subphases.

objects leads to a process of detaching cathexes from these adult objects and investing them in peer objects, a process which promotes the separation-individuation initiated in the first three years of life (Mahler 1965). In man, this detachment and reinvestment of object cathexes stimulated by biology and imposed by civilization, preserves the species. The cathectic transformations serve to make an object of the peer who is able to gratify both affectional and sensual needs. In *Totem and Taboo*, Freud noted that one of the factors leading to the structuralization of the family was the recurrent upsurge of drives and, with these, the need for the object. Against the background of incest taboos and of the Oedipus complex emerges the need for detaching one's original cathexes and finding a genital object-choice not forbidden by civilization: *in adolescence, the heterosexual peer becomes that object.*

This developmental period shows again the fusion of affectional and sensual currents of libido, on the one hand, and their defusion on the other (see Chapter 1). During the phallic phase of development, the genital impulses followed the path of the existing affectional cathexes to the prime love-object generating the first fusion of the two currents of the libido. However, the problems created by the resulting Oedipus complex led to a necessary defusion of these currents of the libido with repression, sublimation, and transformation of part of the sensual cathexis into altruism (A. Freud, 1936). During the latency period defusion was largely maintained as the sensual cathexis was repressed, and later, where it emerged, was generally dealt with autoerotically. Now, as sensual drives are given a new and powerful impetus by pubertal processes, the sensual current cannot remain repressed, except where drastic defenses are brought to bear (to the detriment of total personality development), and socially appropriate objects are sought. This upsurge of genital drive accelerates processes of separation and individuation that lead to devaluation of the affectional cathexes of the parents. Genital cathexes of peers gradually become joined, in late adolescence, with the affectional current, and lead then to more profound and extended object attachments. Certainly, great variation occurs; for example, in the intense "puppy loves" of early and mid-adolescence, the affectional-sensual cathexis of oedipal origin is attached en bloc, even if only transiently to a peer. Optimal love-cathexes of late adolescence tend to consist of fused sensual and affectional currents, so necessary a precondition for mature heterosexual object choice and marriage.

In this context then, we see the great difference in the nature of peer relations during latency and adolescence. Among other characteristics, the cathexis of the peer in latency is less intense, paracentral, and the libidinal currents are essentially defused; in later adolescence the peer cathexis is intense, although it may be short-lived, becomes progressively central, and consists of variable degrees of fused affectional and sensual libido. In adolescence, the *defusion* of the two currents of the libido exists in the relation to the parents: while a reasonable degree of affectional libido remains attached to the object, the reactivated residua of former sensual cathexes are further deposed by repression, displacement, and sublimations. This process sets the stage for the formation of a new object choice. We know that in many cases this does not occur so simply, nor so satisfactorily.

The Needs:

Libidinal—affectional: During adolescence, needs for love, care, and protection begin to be withdrawn from the parents as principal sources of gratification. The affectional libidinal cathexis of the parents following a path similar to that of the genital cathexis, is devalued, although it does not have the same fate. Whereas the genital cathexis is more definitively repressed, sublimated, and/or displaced, the affectional cathexis of the parents may reappear in early adulthood after its relative devaluation in adolescence. The degree of manifest devaluation varies considerably. We usually find extremes of such devaluation in the so-called adolescent rebellion. It would seem that a relative devaluation is essential to optimal individuation and self-reliance. The devaluation invariably proceeds with resistance from existing cathexes. We recall Freud's observation that the organism gives up a libido position only with difficulty. The inevitable dependence-independence conflict of adolescence results as the efforts to individuate come up against the resistance and regressive pull of former cathexes. The struggle is a long one and well known.

The gratification of needs for affectional love during adolescence is sought increasingly from peers, substitute adult objects, and the self. Such needs are gratified by peers in friendships, mutual support, and admiration. Frequent, lengthy telephone calls to each other bear witness to the strength of such needs. To appear like the others, to dress like them particularly evident during early adolescence is determined not only by identity formations, but also, by the need for acceptance and love from the group.

As the organism moves along the developmental line from dependence to self-reliance, we note, as we did earlier, that the superego and ego ideal operate increasingly in the economy of libidinal needs and gratification. The progressive stabilization of psychic structure and of identity formations of late adolescence and young adulthood largely account for the libidinal economics effected and maintained by the self. The subject is now a significant contributor to his own libidinal economy; here is the nucleus of self-reliance. Precisely this latter development, along with processes that have led to altruism, set the stage for the ability "to give", which emerges more and more as adolescence proceeds. Thus, dependence on the object for affectionate love—"to get"—takes on yet another character, being balanced by the increasing ability to altruistically love the object—"to give." This gradual process is significant to becoming an equal partner, anaclitic still and always, but now the *object* of anaclitic cathexes too. Eventually this will prepare for parenthood, when the mode "to give" heavily outweighs that of "to get" (Saul, 1947).

Libidinal–sensual: It is well known that in adolescence sensual needs become dominantly genital and are gratified autoerotically and by the peer. As one moves along in time, and peer objects are sought more actively, autoerotic gratification decreases. With reference to sensual need-gratification, the peer object tends in *early* adolescence to be homosexual. It is doubtful that an affectional cathexis is fused with the sensual one here, and the sensual activity, although reciprocal, is essentially narcissistic. Yet the peer-object may be cathected with affectional libido. One explanation would be that there is still a defusion of sensual and affectional libido and that the sensual cathexis is dominantly narcissistic and insufficiently object-directed.

During the latter two thirds of adolescence, the genital object choice tends to be heterosexual. The sensual cathexis becomes object-directed, and fusion with the affectional current occurs. Although the sensual impulses are powerful, multiple determinants lead usually to brief, unstable cathexes during the beginning of heterosexual object relations of adolescence. With time and further development, the cathexis becomes more stable. While this stabilization of fused affectional and sensual cathexes is taking place, autoerotic paths of discharge-gratification are still used. Autoerotism is selected because, among other factors, as pressing as the impulses are, they cannot ignore superego reaction or external prohibitions. Of course, differences occur in the vicissitudes of sensual need-gratification in boys and girls; it did so earlier and will do so in adolescence and thereafter.

It may well be that the stability of the heterosexual object choice is dependent on the stability of the affectional cathexis and on the object-directedness of the sensual one. Certainly, the sensual cathexis largely determines the object choice; i. e., the object must be attractive and satisfactory to sensual impulses, compatible with sensual fantasies arising from id cathexes, before those impulses become attached to that object representation. Frequently, a subject is attracted to an object by the power of the sensual cathexis aroused by visual and other stimulation as well as fantasies. Approach to the object and tentative object relations then allow for attachment of affectional cathexis, and the formation of a fused libidinal object relationship follows. Variations are, of course, numerous; some objects are used simply for the gratification of a sensual need. In other cases, sensual—particularly genital—gratification serves the gratification of dependent needs for love, attention, protection, or other needs. On the other hand, genitality in early adolescence, by reactivating oedipal fantasies, often leads to regression. These regressions, generally along psychosexual epigenetic lines, lead to oral and anal sensual need-discharge mechanisms which influence the character of need-gratification and dependence on objects. A not unusual example of such regression is that of the 14-year-old who, in seven months, gains 80 pounds. Some mechanisms may appear as a defense not only against genitality, but also against dependence on the object, often, but not always, in the service of separation-individuation and autonomy. Many permutations exist.

Ego—developmental: Dependence on teachers and parents for education and development of skills continues in adolescence. The need for adult as well as peer models for further identity formation is significant. A boy must wear the same style trousers and shirt, adopt the same haircut as his friends. Reasonable ego and superego restructuralizations and modifications depend largely on the balance and judicious shifts in limit-setting and freedoms exercised by parents, particularly the father. The peer group also exerts considerable pressure in setting limits and dictating conduct. Of course, the peer group also exerts pressure from the side of the impulses; nor can we fail to mention the unconscious pressures frequently exerted by parents from this same side.

Regarding self-reliance, the ego, in conjunction with demands from the superego, acquires more and more responsibility for protecting the self against internal and external dangers. Often in late adolescence, protection of the self is increasingly provided by religious ideas, a system which may become structured autonomously or is carried over from upbringing. These constructs, in many instances, are rejected at this period along with other parent representations and parent-related Weltanschauungen. Where religious ideas are accepted, they emerge as a result of the externalization of archaic psychic representations of objects and their functions which afford psychic protection as did the idealized parents of infancy. Since these constructs arise from intrapsychic sources, we may consider them to arise in the service of autonomy and to insure self-reliance. Yet it would seem, paradoxically, the externalization of these archaic representations only demonstrates man's unyielding dependence on the object. Group factors are, of course, operative here, as are many intrapsychic ones.

The Objects:

Most significant for further psychic development is the dissolution of the primacy of the parents as love objects, protectors, caretakers. Duties and responsibilities carried by these objects begin to be withdrawn from them in adolescence, at least in specific areas. Gradually, the heterosexual peer begins to receive the fused cathexis which is so vital to a mature marriage. Much stabilization of this fused cathexis will occur before a stable mate-choice can be made. The roles of the parent and of the peer as love object undergo significant modification in adolescence: in a sense, the first loses what the second gains.

The parents' function of protector also decreases, although not as significantly as that of love object. The parent is still needed for protection, but here too, much is taken over by the self. Often, as noted before, religious belief takes up this function; in some areas it is society. Need for parental care-taking which, in western civilization extends through late adolescence, is a frequent source of conflict because this dependence encounters strong wishes and emotional readiness for "total" self-reliance.

On the other hand, we believe that, in adolescence particularly, too vigorous defenses against dependence on the object for gratification of libidinal needs may lead to as serious problems for further development as may too great dependence on objects.

We have emphasized that the peer relations of adolescence vary notably in character from those of the latency phase. We believe it of great importance that the adolescent peer provides opportunities for fusion of the affectional and sensual currents of the libido, a process highly desirable for the next phase of development.

EARLY ADULTHOOD

Epigenetic Issues:

Separation from the parental home, living on one's own are effected generally during this decade. So is marriage and the beginning of parenthood. These tasks, when achieved satisfactorily, represent great developments of the psychic organization. The degree of growth that occurs can perhaps best be realized by considering that this decade forms the bridge between adolescence and mature adulthood, from the 18-year-old adolescent to the 32-year-old man or woman, from the single student to the married man, breadwinner, and parent (Saul, 1967). This is for many, with the exception of old age, the period of greatest although temporary isolation. This is the period of greatest autonomy to date, and one which most tests self-reliance. It is the period during which still higher degrees of identity formation jell, particularly with reference to selection of work, professional identity; here, philosophic and religious Weltanschauungen consolidate.

The equation of the affectional current of the libido, "to get"⇌"to give" shifts further to the right with the selection of a mate, a shift still further accentuated with parenthood. The offspring's needs call for this shift which may well be determined by instinctive-experiential interlockings (Benedek, 1949; Saul, 1947; Saul and Pulver, 1965). As we noted in Chapter 2, the altriciality of the human neonate requires an *auxiliary ego* for its survival. That homo-sapiens has survived bears evidence to the fact that the auxiliary ego is guaranteed, a guarantee which probably has maternal, parenting, IRM's interlocking with childhood identifications and learning.

The Needs:

Libidinal—affectional: Leaving home often leads to insecurity which taxes the psychic organization. Psychic equilibrium between ego and superego, and between ego and ego ideal, along with stabilized object constancy and identity formations, are the great contributors to inner sustainment and thence to self-reliance. Nevertheless, external sources of libidinal gratification are needed, and are in large part the result of early life-conditioning and man's resultant anaclitic (or symbiotic) condition, as well as of the age-adequate anaclitic character of certain need-gratifications. The insecurity of the early part of this period of relative isolation which may be characterized by insufficient gratification of anaclitic needs is often felt as loneliness and depression. Objects can and do provide protection, care, and indulgence, as well as advice, encouragement, and companionship. So does society which, for example, makes efforts to protect against law-breaking. For many, religion also becomes—if it has not been—a source of love, care, and protection; for others, this source of need-gratification is now abandoned.

The heterosexual peer becomes the prime external source of libidinal need-gratification, and we see here phenomena strongly reminiscent of emotional refueling albeit at a much higher level of psychosocial development: for example, the phone calls, the letters when separated, and the like.

Libidinal—sensual: The intense cathexis of the object which is experienced by the ego as a need reaches maximal intensity at this period. The genital cathexis achieves stable fusion with the affectional current of the libido. Often now, the genital cathexis carries with it the affectional current; as the body of the sperm seems followed by its tail. The seeking of the object by the genital cathexis obtains the greatest degree of freedom during this developmental period, and thus the genital needs are unbridled and consciously experienced. The character of these impulses no longer produce the anxieties they caused the adolescent ego (A. Freud, 1936) under the impact of the dread of the impulses, the threatening dissolution of the ego, and the often too loud or too silent superego. Now the character of the psychic organization is vastly more stabilized and inherently consistent, both in terms of structural stability and identity formations.

The fused, or principally genital, cathexis is subject to the vicissitudes of meeting the object, courting the object, and contract formation (object-relation). With this, all the uncertainties and anxieties surrounding success and fear of rejection tend to intensify and may lead to defense against the need for the object. Where such anxiety is too great, it will interfere with optimal gratifications and object relations. Autoerotism generally succumbs to the greater imperative of gratification by the object; as a source of gratification, autoerotism serves now, more than heretofore, but as a temporizing measure.

Ego—developmental: Dependence on teachers is still great in those striving for professional identity, less so for laborers. In the partnership of marriage and parenthood, advice, consultation, and support are often sought from seniors or peer objects.

The Objects:

Separation from home is often dealt with by maintaining ties with the peer group or forming new ones. From the group, several peers may be selected to whom object-specific cathexes are attached. The search for the hetero-sexual peer, potential mate, takes on a task-characteristic. Once the mate-object is found, peers and parents will grad-ually recede to more peripheral object positions in part due to the energy-binding of the libidinal cathexis of the mate. If the cathexis attached to the mate in the early phase of marriage is not seriously impeded by neurotic conflict, that cathexis will stabilize and the object relation consolidate (Saul, 1967).

We believe too that in many instances the affectional cathexis of the parents re-emerges following some stabiliza-tion of the heterosexual cathexis of marriage. In other cases, the parents continue to be displaced from high-valence cathexis and do not form a close part of the new family group. There are, of course, many variations.

With the advent of pregnancy and parenthood, an in-tense object cathexis attaches to the newborn. During this period, the "to get"$\rightleftharpoons$"to give" equation of the libido shifts sharply still further to the right. Many factors, of course, influence the character of the cathexis of the mate and of the offspring; it may well be that those cathexes of the offspring vary in male and female.

As has been noted already, need-gratifications continue to be provided by parents, society, objects in a group, and, for many, by religion.

MIDDLE ADULTHOOD

Epigenetic Issues:

Stability of the personality and of object relations is maximal during this long period of life's trajectory. Immaturity obstructs such stability, since it leads to insufficient differentiation of identity formations and psychic structure; it also entails insufficient changes in psychic energy which unfavorably affect the economy of libido and aggression. Intrapsychic conflicts do not allow for optimal inner sustainment and object cathexes, causing both to be unstable. It is well known that some immaturity and intrapsychic—and resulting interpersonal—conflict are ubiquitous in adult man. War and hostilities in the world, the inability of the poor to rise above poverty bear witness to this broad assumption.

Setting aside considerations of immaturities, the healthy adult is generally subject to periods of need, conscious and unconscious. This may be expressed in libidinal life itself, in object relations, in work and professional status, or in relation to goals and ambitions. At the same time, one cannot underestimate the degree of man's self-reliance, of the competence with which he has organized the sources of his need-gratifications.

The degree to which the adult can remain oblivious to his "anaclitic" life condition is remarkable, as the following incident shows. One of the authors was in conference with two women engaged in the psychotherapy of children. Both were approximately the same age (40) and of similar situation, but for the fact that one woman's husband had become seriously ill. The discussion turned to object relations and the child's need for the object. In a further turn, the issue became personalized. While the first therapist commented with justified pleasure on her independence, the second (with the seriously ill husband) began to cry, upon which the first suddenly became sober. She stopped talking as the full impact of her vulnerability became apparent to her: what if her husband were to suddenly become seriously ill, his life threatened?

It is not so clear what the fate is of the dependent needs—at the core of which lie the libidinal needs of the infantile in us all (Saul, 1947)—in the adult who lives alone. It may be too simple an assumption to consider that the adult who is living alone necessarily has unmet needs for love, sex, companionship, protection, and support. We know of many instances where needs for companionship, affection, and even protection are transferred to animals. We mentioned earlier the displacement of dependent need-gratifications, i. e., the displacement and modification of object-libido to a house, institution, or neighborhood (not always in the sense of altruism); the substitution of dependence "on what" for "on whom." Variants of this process of displacement and modification of need for libidinal gratification from objects are also seen in the adult living alone who expends his efforts and derives gratification from achievements in his work and thereby makes a contribution to society and civilization.

The Needs:

Libidinal—Affectional: Stability in the adult psychic and environmental structures includes a stabilizing of need gratification: sources of love, care, and protection are essentially assigned. For example, one person will rely on religion for partial gratification of these needs; another will distribute his expectations more heavily to other Weltanschauungen—perhaps art and science—and/or to other sources such as the self, objects, and society (see Freud, 1930, Chapter 2). Many people have shared the experience of libidinal gratification as did Franz von Schober, in the following lines from his poem "To Music," immortalized by Schubert; *Du holde Kunst, in wie viel grauen Stunden,*

Wo mich des Lebens wilder Kreis umstrickt, has du mein Herz zu warmer Lieb entzunden, hast mich in eine bess're Welt entrueckt.[4] (Schubert, 1895, p. 238).

Libidinal—Sensual: Unless obstructed by immaturities and intrapsychic conflict, these are generally gratified by the mate.

Nonlibidinal: Here self-reliance is manifest to its greatest degree. However, in areas of skill-specialization, many an adult is a student and continues to learn from more skilled seniors. Another manifestation of dependence in the adult arises from needs for care and protection as occurs in illness; these needs are met by turning to the doctor. Or the attorney is consulted in a matter of law. Other needs come under care and protection and occur in relation to "external" realities. In our field, adults consult us on how to best cope with problems in themselves and in their children.

The Objects:

Adult object relations have become quite complex. Although satisfactory inner sustainment is the *sine qua non* of well-being, man continues to require the object to gratify most of his libidinal needs. On the other hand, no amount of external support and love can guarantee security in the adult, when inner sustainment is poor. We are speaking of the economy of libido. Objects, the sources of libido from without, are multiple. The love-object, the

[4]Thou lovely art, in so many gray hours
when trapped in life's many crises
you have roused my heart to greater love,
you have taken me to a better world.
(Translated by H. P.)

mate of the adult dyad is imbued with and returns fused affectional and sensual libido. Friends and parents obtain and provide affectional libido. The subject's children are the recipients of large portions of affectional libido, but as they grow they begin to provide affectional libido too, and in addition, can gratify and raise narcissistic libido in the parents. Investments in the community can lead to "being loved" and protected by the group. As mentioned above, some libidinal gratification comes from art and various forms of entertainment.

LATE ADULTHOOD

Epigenetic Issues:

At the time of writing this chapter, one of the authors received a letter from a close friend whose husband had died a year earlier. Her statement so well describes the life-condition at this phase that here, with permission, we quote a few passages:

> I had a very, very hard year, giving up the big house, disposing, selling, distributing every single piece of our belongings of our long life together. . . . I finally found an apartment I knew I would like to live in, quite near our old house. . . . I am still working . . . as long as they don't kick me out, due to being (as they call it) over-age. I dread that, for that will make me feel and be old, when I have to stop working. I do practice the piano quite a bit now, hoping to do chamber music. My family gives me *much* pleasure, . . . I lost my brother . . . and also M.'s brother L. this year. You see how urgently I need to work in order to be busy and not lonely. That is why I said I had such a hard year but I try hard to manage to keep my balance with all the *inner* happiness I have accumulated over the years, and that which is still coming from *outside* (italics added).

At no time in adulthood will self-reliance and inner sustainment more determine the well-being of the individual than now. But both are subjected to the harsh vicissitudes of aging. Self-reliance is attacked from two directions—loss of objects, particularly of the mate, leads to necessary readjustments in need-gratification constellations and even patterning; and the biology of aging leads to a reduction in individual capabilities.

Inner sustainment is attacked at this period particularly by the vicissitudes of self-esteem. Where self-esteem is still largely based on infantile narcissistic residua, the subject will suffer from self-devaluations accompanying aging. The most reliable source of self-esteem, that provided by the ego's achievements and capabilities, are significantly determined by the individual's work. At this period of life, loss of a job or enforced retirement deal many a heavy blow, resulting in severe self-devaluation. Vigorous men and women, active until "retirement age," may rapidly deteriorate both physically and emotionally after relinquishing work. Many die within one or two years of retirement. Their need to be useful, respected, important to those about them is unequivocal. Women, because their feeling of usefulness is in large part associated with procreation, may encounter this problem earlier, in the menopause. Those who do not have a great degree of body narcissism are more fortunate in that the changes of menopause come about when "aging bodily-changes," so notable later, are less evident. Thus they may deal with one aging process at a time and sustain narcissistic devaluation more gradually. Their loss of self-esteem may be, generally speaking, less global than in men, allowing reparative and adaptive mechanisms to be set more easily to work. Where men and women have reached satisfactory levels of emotional maturity, in Saul's sense (1947, 1965 with Pulver), they will have prepared for the eventualities of decreasing bodily function, suffer less narcissistic devaluation by aging processes and maintain "integrity" of ego functioning and ego identity, in Erikson's (1959) sense. The core of self-esteem, and with it of inner sustainment, resides most securely in the adaptive functioning of the ego and the maintenance of the "integrity" of identity formations.

The third source of self-esteem, gratification of object love, of the need to be loved, Freud observed (1930, p. 82), to be the source with the greatest vulnerability. Object loss and mourning is the inevitable consequence of object love. With object loss attaining its peak frequency now, grief and mourning, expensive procedures in terms of psychic economy, seriously threaten self-esteem equilibria. In addition, the daily gratifications that accrue from the interaction with the love object are no longer available. For many people this period is one of isolation and deep libidinal impoverishment.

Self-esteem is thus subject to depletion by narcissistic devaluation and diminution in ego functions that allowed for earlier achievements and self-reliance. In addition, unsolicited gratification of object love may be lost, decreasing libidinal supplies and further depleting self-esteem. Inner sustainment upholding self-reliance may be insufficient. One of the usual paths of refueling inner sustainment conditioned from infancy, is to turn to the external sources of supply and support. These, however, are less available now, so that this path to gratification, too, is often cut off.

During this period of life, inner sustainment depends mostly on "the integrity" of ego functioning and identity formation (Erikson, 1959). A contribution to that sustainment comes also from the capacity to be alone, in Winnicott's sense, alone with one's internalized love objects (ob-

ject-constancy). The most reliable condition for maintenance of inner sustainment comes from one's own continued creative activities.

The emotionally mature man will have accepted over
the years the inevitable termination of his own life cycle
(Erikson 1959). Psychic defenses against this self-confron-
tation are, of course, often used. Where such acceptance or
defense fails, despair (Erikson, 1959) is inevitable, intensi-
fying the need for support from without. In addition to
leading to regressions, despair may, by way of depression-
withdrawal (Engel, 1962), add its weight to the side of
aging physiologic processes and accelerate somatic illness
and death.

The Needs:

Libidinal—affectional: Needs for love may increase over
those of the previous long period of adulthood, as threat
of loss or, actual loss of the mate and other objects make
existing needs felt more intensely. The character of inner
sustainment will determine the intensity of need-gratification sought from without.

Libidinal—sensual: Sensual needs are perhaps even more
variable than before. We know little of the status of sensual needs at this age period. Many factors, as always, influence the status of these needs. Waning of such needs, in
some cases, is associated with physiologic aging processes
and organic disorders.

Nonlibidinal: Because of physiologic aging, organic de-
generative and pathologic processes, the needs for care and
protection now generally increase. Again the auxiliary ego
of another object is more or less needed. For example, it is
not unusual for a greater degree of dependence to develop

on the physician, and other health-caring persons. Prototypes for such dependence come from childhood experiences. Self-neglect is not uncommon among isolates of this
age group.

The Object:

Isolation and loneliness are direct reflections of absence
of objects. Again, inner sustainment and existing object
relations determine the condition of the subject's psychic
state. Unquestionably, as Freud so frequently observed
from 1926 on, man, influenced in such large measure by
his earliest conditioning during the prolonged period of
childhood dependence, is eminently ill equipped to face
life alone.

CONCLUSION

Using the developmental line "from dependency to
emotional self-reliance and adult object-relationships" (A.
Freud, 1963) and Mahler's (1965) profile for separation-
individuation, we have attempted to formulate an epigenesis of psychologic dependence. We now recapitulate by
presenting highlights of each coordinate of dependence in
continuity rather than by developmental phase.

The Needs:

We have attempted to delineate the needs in broad categories. No effort is made to isolate one need from the
others; rather, categories overlap, and needs occur in fused,
amalgamated forms.

We have noted that *physiological* needs are cyclic, constant and undergo very little modification except during the first two years of life. In describing *libidinal* needs, we find it very useful to follow the concept of two currents of the libido: affectional and sensual. The *affectional* needs for protection, care and indulgence emerge during the normal symbiosis in the first half-year of life, and are perpetual. Intensity of these needs is determined by the economy of the libido and by the development of the psychic organization. A complementary relationship exists between inner sustainment and sustainment from without. The infant whose scarcely-differentiated psychic organization provides little libidinal sustainment from within depends greatly on the object for sustainment.

The *sensual* needs have been much described in concepts of psychosexual development. The first experiences of mouth, skin, and proprioceptive erotism are narcissistic and auto-erotic, whereas, later, sensuality is essentially object-directed and represents the fundamental differentiation of Eros. The emergence of phallic-genitality makes its great contributions to the development of psychic structure and to individuation while undergoing repression and sublimation. Genitality is biphasic, a condition unique to man, according to present knowledge, with the period of latency interposed between the two peaks of activity, the phallic-oedipal phase and puberty. Latency manifests itself as a period of repression and suppression of genital impulses. The upsurge of genitality at puberty initiates adult sexuality. Allowing for wide variations, genital activity tends to wane during the last phase of life.

In contrast, the *affectional* needs, after a marked peak during the normal symbiotic phase, tend to remain at a relatively constant level of intensity throughout life and do not wane during the last years; indeed, they may even rise at that time because of physiologic and psychologic aging factors.

Ego-developmental needs represent the nonlibidinal psychic dependence on environmental stimuli and the co-ordinating object which the individual experiences in adapting to his internal and external milieux. The development of the ego parallels the development of self-reliance; i. e., the more the ego can determine the subject's destiny autonomously, the greater the subject's self-reliance.

In terms of adaptation, ego-developmental dependence is greatest at birth. Need for auxiliary-ego activity decreases from the normal symbiotic phase onward and reaches its minimal level in adulthood. With late adulthood, auxiliary-ego needs—and dependence—rise again as the ego is subjected to aging processes.

Changes occur in the qualities and priorities of need throughout the process of maturation and development. Fluctuations in intensity of specific needs appear at different periods. For example, being frightened intensifies the need for protection; being sexually stimulated leads to sensual tensions, and the search for gratification becomes urgent; having to make a decision induces, in many people, the need for counsel.

"To Get"⇌"To Give"

Our schema may not sufficiently emphasize the importance of the change in vector of libidinal transaction. Thus, the infant relates in a libidinal mode best characterized by Saul (1947) and Erikson (1950, 1959) as the mode "to get"—to be loved, to be protected. As the individual develops, he is able "to give" to others. A large step in this direction is taken with the development of altruism which occurs with the resolution of the Oedipus complex; elements of such altruism in the affectional current of the libido make their appearance earlier, perhaps, as precursors (see Chapter 1). With latency, the libidinal equation "to get"⇌"to give" shifts further to the right. In adolescence, the equation arrives at an equilibrium midpoint between the two. Principally, it is expressed in alternations of needs "to get" and needs "to give," at a period when shifts of dependence and self-reliance are great. With young adulthood and stabilization of the psychic organization, altruism and the ability "to give" increase and stabilize further. Marriage, and particularly parenthood, lead to a sharp shift of the equation to the right. The character of inner sustainment and of the libidinal relation of marital partners are the principal pillars that make possible and sustain optimal parental "giving."

The shift of the libidinal equation to the right is never complete, or at least never for long during adulthood. In late adulthood, the equation may tend to shift back toward center, or further to the left, as inner sustainment and object relations are both challenged by aging processes.

Object relations

The love object is first experienced in the child-mother dyad. Dependence on the object is pervasive and the mode is "to get" from the object, at first passively and then actively. The earliest relation to the father is dyadic as well and parallels that of the child-mother relation. Soon some differentiation of role and function is ascribed to each parent. Generally, the mother nurtures, the father protects and sets limits. Of course much overlap of function occurs and, in effect, both parents are seen as sources of protection, care, and indulgence.

With the progression of psychosexual development, of differentiation of libido and of separation-individuation, object relations acquire an added dimension: they become triadic, with the development of the Oedipus complex. The conflicts created here lead to necessary modifications in investment of libido in the parents. The genital libido is detached from the love object and, by its modification, contributes to the development of the affectional current of the libido. Among the changes this brings about is the addition of concern for others: of altruism.

With powerful efforts to suppress the expression of genitality during latency, we suggest that there is a (relative) defusion of affectional and sensual libido, resulting in object relations being preponderantly cathected with affectional libido. The horizon of object relations has expanded, and the peer, in many instances the same-sex peer, becomes a significant object. Often, earlier peer relations with siblings occur, but the relation to the nonsibling peer differs in important respects from the rivalrous peer relation of sibship. For one thing, the cathected latency peer is an object with more reciprocal altruistic capabilities and functions than is the rivalrous sibling. During latency a dichotomy exists between the cathexis of the peer and the parent; but both tend to be cathected principally with affectional libido, the genital libido being under great pressure by the ego not to become expressed.

We point particularly to the great difference between the peer of latency and the peer of adolescence. In adolescence, under the influence of the upsurge of genitality resulting from and initiated by puberty, the peer becomes cathected with gradually greater degrees of fused affectional and genital libido. With this development, the heterosexual peer object obtains great significance and makes possible the second round of detachment of cathexes from adult love-objects and childhood attachments to the parents. These, of course, enhance the continuance of the individuation process. Self-reliance is further engendered when these processes proceed successfully. The heterosexual peer substitutes in part for the parents. The parents, however, are still needed for significant care and protection.

Achievement of cathexis of the heterosexual, adolescent peer prepares the way for the selection of a mate. With marriage and parenthood the subject arrives at the adult phase, the longest in life's trajectory, and—except for the symbiosis of infancy where security and stability were supreme—generally the most stable. In late adulthood, natural processes lead to object loss, and a return to isolation occurs with loss of the mate. Sustainment from within, at this juncture especially, is of great importance to sustaining life.

PART III

CLINICAL CONSIDERATIONS

6. Some Clinical Aspects of Dependence

If dependence is present throughout life, if it is rooted in man's earliest psychic experiences, what, then, are the consequences? We here describe some of the vicissitudes of dependence in symptom and character formation, some of the dynamics of reactive dependence, and some of the ways man adapts to his dependent needs.

Infantile dependence is at first passive; soon it becomes active and, therewith, adaptive. Complementarily, parents enhance the development of the "confident expectation" (Benedek, 1949) that they can be depended upon, which leads to the development of the child's affection for them. Freud (1940) suggested that the mother arouses the child's sexuality by her caring, parental ministrations, by stimulating erotogenic zones, and partly gratifying sexual impulses. This concept can be extended to the area of dependence as well. By gratifying needs and providing pleasure, by behavior that will lead to the development of basic trust and object constancy, the mother arouses and gratifies yearnings to be loved and cared for.

We know that being loved is pleasurable and gratifying in itself, that it becomes the psychologic representative of security. Freud remarked (1930, Chapter II) that although man is most vulnerable in his dependence on objects, he has made love from those objects the central method of attaining happiness.

DEPENDENCE AND CHARACTER DISORDERS

The importance to survival of dependence in infancy and childhood leaves its mark. One of the most dramatic problems in dependence presents in symbiotic childhood psychosis (Mahler, 1952; Mahler and Gosliner, 1955) where the psychologic dependence is extreme. Psychic fusion between self and object, characteristic of normal symbiosis, remains fixated in symbiotic childhood psychosis. Indeed, the panic engendered by separation bespeaks the intensity of the dependence. In contrast, the even more serious problem of infantile autism reflects the price paid for *not recognizing "that help comes from the outside"* (Mahler, 1952), that is, for remaining oblivious to the existence of the object on whom the child is in reality dependent. (Here, we believe that constitution as well as upbringing plays its part.) Symbiotic childhood psychosis and infantile autism underline the thesis that the origins of reasonable socialization arise from the child's dependence on others for protection, care, and love. In autism as in certain antisocial character disorders, we see the disastrous effects of not valuing the dependence on the object. These disorders show us that valuing the object's love makes age-adequate dependence on the object a most adaptive and salutary phenomenon.

Of course, problems of insufficient or excessive dependence do not occur just in childhood. Thus the "oral-dependent" character well known to every clinician shows a prominence of age-excessive dependent behavior. Saul has elsewhere (1947) elaborated on the dynamics of one type of dependent character (frequently found among both men and women). Such a person, if a man, tries to live up to ideals of self-reliance, but is in fact notably dependent and unconsciously resents the demands made on him by his wife, children, and job. He defends against these inner feelings by putting on a great show of superiority. Any significant task or responsibility leads to regression, to dependence which in turn leads to loss of self-esteem and anger, so that he becomes difficult, weak, and boastful.

The hysterical character often exhibits regressive dependent behavior, resulting from both fixation at pregenital levels of development, and the wish to obtain gratification of drive derivatives from the phallic level of psychosexual development against which the dependent behavior is a defense (regression, denial, substitution.)

As we have already observed, problems of insufficient dependence on objects are as difficult as those arising from excessive dependence. With antisocial character disorders in which insufficient dependence on objects exists, the cathexis of the object and of the object's love is depreciated as a result of which the dictates of the object lose their valence or have not become internalized. In these cases, insufficient dependence may arise from constitutional defect, but can usually be traced to protracted excessive frustration of childhood dependent needs.

Excessive dependence is readily accepted as a common denominator in alcoholism and drug addiction, where the alcohol, the drug is substituted for the object. Substitution of dependence "on whom" for "on what" seems clear enough. But the line between dependence "on whom", or "on what" and dependence "for what" blurs: the subject is dependent "on" alcohol and "for" alcohol. This suggests a condensation wherein the same substance handles both co-ordinates of dependence. Although love from the object is craved manifestly; the object, in many such cases, has undergone devaluation and has been substituted for. It would seem plausible that this alcohol or drug substitution attempts to compensate for the devalued object which has insufficient or inconstant influence on the economy of the libido. Thus the object has insufficient positive influence in the gratification dynamics of the subject. It should be quite clear that we make this observation to suggest but one thread in the complex fabric of alcoholism and drug addiction. It may well be that, among the severe determinants that make alcoholism and drug addiction so difficult to treat, is the fact that the devaluation of objects makes these ineffectual in gratifying the dependent needs of the subject, and often ineffectual as media for treatment. We have little doubt that the reactive substitution of the chemical for the object as source of gratification is among the genetic determinants of these conditions.

In a similar dynamic but not such a characterologic picture, a crisis situation can lead to such substitutive sources of gratification. An attractive, intelligent young woman reacted to her husband's leaving her for another woman with depression, sporadic overdrinking and overeating which invariably occurred in association with excessive feelings of loneliness.

REACTIVE DEPENDENCE

We have emphasized that dependence is the product of the organism's altriciality. We have suggested that, hand in hand with altriciality, Eros itself (Freud, 1920), unequivocally one of the most powerful forces in living organisms determines the dependence of one organism on another. We add here that anxiety—helplessness of the ego—is the principal determinant of *reactive* psychologic dependence. This is not reserved for man alone. Harlow's monkeys showed such reactive dependence on their inanimate surrogate "mothers" in the presence of a novel stimulus (Chapter 2). In that situation, the behavior of the infant monkeys showed the effects of the object's power to decrease fear and even to endow the infant with the wherewithall to explore the threatening ("monster toy") stimulus. The frightened young seeking out the protecting parent is commonly seen in animal young. We have, of course, seen the same reactive dependence occurring in interspecies object relations, which is consonant with the interspecies attachment described by ethologists (Chapter 2). Reactive dependence is readily observable in domesticated animals.

Wish for Parental Care and
Protection Reactive to Insecurity

Howard M., a young law clerk, came to analysis while still a student because he realized that his extreme diffidence about speaking before audiences would interfere

with his career. Many problems relating to his dependent
needs appeared during the course of his analysis. Late in
the analysis, when the transference was well established,
he told of his fantasy that the analyst would call one of
the partners in his firm to secure for him a·particular brief
which would give him a rare chance to prove himself. His
associations indicated not only that his fantasy expressed
his infantile belief that the parent had the power to manipulate the environment, but that he equated the analyst's
intervention on his behalf with love.

Every analyst encounters this demand that he exercise omnipotent powers the patient wishes he had.
Another patient, the mother of two children, whose
husband had recently left her for another woman,
asked the analyst to call in her husband to talk to
him, ostensibly so he could know more about her. It
became clear that she wanted the analyst to talk the
husband into returning to her.

Similarly, a nine-year-old boy, who had just received a
"brain-toy" with which one matches wits, patience and
skill, was disappointed that his father could not get a
perfect score. In fact, he was certain that his father
would. This conviction that the father has remarkable
powers leads the child to expect that father can help
him, extricate him from troubles, and even manipulate
the environment for him.

The need for the power of the parent, of course, also
emerges in connection with dangers. Parents are protectors against external as well as internal dangers, real
and fantasied. This ingredient of dependence on an all-
powerful parent is most conspicuous in religion (See
Chapter 1).

The Need for Love and Support
Reactive to Loss of Self-Esteem

The need to be loved (complement to the fear of loss of love of the danger-situation series) is ubiquitous from the time of its emergence as a psychologic force in the first years of life. Whatever biologic determinants of dependence may exist, the need to be loved, in large part arises from conditioning experiences in the normal symbiotic relationship with the mother; as Erikson might have it (1959, p. 60), it arises from an economic deficit associated with the gradual dissolution of that symbiosis, the then-lost paradise. Affectional love corrects loss of self-esteem, feelings of being small and inadequate, it gratifies narcissistic wishes to be admired and respected. It gives value—libido—to the self and insures the stability of identity formations. Love from without may outrank superego criticism, although we know it often does not, particularly in cases with large degrees of guilt.

During his analysis, Howard M. failed his bar examination and then had this dream. "Concrete breasts are crushing my brain ... it's like torture in a P.O.W. camp." He recognized his intense need for love, although he showed marked resistence to using the word. He saw the connection between this need and the loss in self-esteem arising from his academic failure. The breasts of concrete are, of course, ungiving. His analyst had been ill and could not see him. Therefore, he perceived the analyst as ungiving, and was angry with him. But to be angry with the analyst repeated the risk of not being loved by his mother. The anger is then turned against himself: the breast is not only ungiving, but will crush his brain (highly cathected organ). He turned against himself the anger which arose from the blow to his residual narcissistic omnipotence and depreciation of ego achievements. And he attempted to re-establish his libidinal equilibrium by getting love from the analyst, the transference love-object.

The analyst was not the only object from whom he sought love and support. He turned also to his wife and to a particular colleague. His wife, he said, comforted him when she saw he was hurt. He wrote a letter to his friend from whom, he recognized, he was asking support in the form of a statement: "We expect great things from you."

After the analytic session following the news of his failure, the patient felt manifestly better. He felt intensely his dependence on the analyst although it required all the courage he could muster to acknowledge it to himself. We see here how reaction to the recognition of his dependence on the analyst contributed to his feeling small, to a narcissistic blow, and to shame. Loss of self-esteem led to a sharp increment in the need for love, support, and respect from objects. In this case, it led to adaptive behavior. The mode of securing gratification of his needs was to actively seek it out from available objects. Frustration of dependent love needs, intensified further in the analytic situation because the analyst had been ill, led to feelings of deprivation (concrete breasts) and anger, here turned against the self (crushing brain . . . torture). Anger was turned against the self because of the fear of further loss of love from the transference-object during what was a critical libido-depleted period. While recovering from his failure to pass his bar examination, Howard M. reported a dream: "I am at a pool with, I believe, my wife, the image of the person is vague. I dive from the edge of the pool, a very long dive, I am soaring. Very pleased with the achievement." The affect in the dream is "pleasure, satisfaction." He was uncertain whether the onlooker was proud, envious, or both. Associations revealed a strong wish to be admired for a recent achievement. He experienced competitive feelings with regard to his analyst. His need for admiration led to a shame-guilt sequence. The wish to be admired produced shame because his yearnings both revealed to him his feelings of inadequacy, his need for love from others, as well as his hostile competition with people whom he admired and respected. This self-image was ego-alien and caused a diminution in self-esteem.

Fear of Loss of Father's Love Reactive to Competition with Him

In analysis, our young lawyer's oedipal rivalry manifested itself by feelings of competitiveness with the analyst. He wished he had the analyst's fantasied wealth, that he were the analyst instead of the patient. His prime anxiety was that the analyst would retaliate by not wanting to see him anymore, by withdrawing his interest (transference love). This transiently gave place to identification with the idealized analyst, in the wish to act as he felt the analyst would act and to be protective of his son and wife.

For a long period in analysis, the anxiety created by hostile competitiveness came in large part from the fear of loss of the father—by abandonment—and of his love. It was fear of loss of love from the admired father that seemed pre-eminent in working through the competitiveness, in wanting to be like father, rather than to take father's place. It is true that the competition was not for an object

(i. e., the analyst's wife) but rather for the idealized stature and achievements of the father figure.

Thus, one of the prime movers in the resolution of competition with father in this man was found by reconstruction to be fear of loss of love from the loved and admired father. Of great importance too, were the young man's love feelings for his father which added to the side of the forces in favor of giving up the competition. For Freud, as we noted in Chapter 1, the dynamics of the Oedipus complex continued to evolve. From 1924 on, he made a distinction between the development and resolution of the Oedipus complex in boys and girls. He suggested that in boys the fear of castration and in girls the fear of loss of love from the object, deal the blow to the oedipal strivings. We saw, in Howard M., whose identity was clearly masculine, the large part played in the resolution of his Oedipus complex by fear of loss of love from the loved and admired father, with whom he competed but also identified. Freud (1926, Chapter IV and VII) noted this in relation to little Hans. Of course, on the same side for giving up the Oedipus, was the pre-eminent castration fear. Concerning the resolution of the Oedipus complex, Waelder stated: "The only causes of its destruction in the female sex [is] privation and dread of loss of love, while in boys castration anxiety is *another contributing factor*" (1937, p. 430, our italics).

Fear of Loss of Mother's Love Reactive to the Expression of Sensual Impulses

Richard B., a young man of 23, presented with a study inhibition and transient impotence only with girls he liked. He had not masturbated from the age of 12 to 18. The precipitating event was seeing his mother naked in the bathroom. Dreams and associations revealed fear of being found masturbating by his father, with consequent mutilation fears. He discovered then a masturbatory fantasy that included his mother as love object. It subsequently emerged that he was mother's favorite and that she indicated in no uncertain terms that sex was filthy and undesirable. He feared that if she discovered he masturbated she would stop loving him. He thus feared punishment by his father but, even more imposingly, feared he would lose his mother's love in retribution for having sexual feelings. The power of the need for love from his mother led to his denying sexual feelings at a time when sexual impulses are so imperative. He also denied any pleasure at a "dirty joke," at pictures of naked women, and did not allow the sensual cathexis to be displaced onto an appropriate peer object. He had to deny sexual arousal per se. Dependent love needs took precedence over sexual strivings. When, at 18, he eventually turned to girls sexually, he intermittently repressed sexual arousal with those in whom he became "interested." For a time, during treatment, he was rejected by his girl; his overriding reaction was the dread that she would stop loving him, he became impotent. When this period passed and he was no longer impotent, he became depressed. Working through that depression gave evidence that he was mourning the mother as object for both affectional and sensual feelings.

In this young man the sensual cathexis was paralyzed by the intense fear of loss of mother's love. In part it was because the mother and then the boy's superego considered sex objectionable. In brief, he could not have mother's love and approval if he also had sexual feelings; he therefore set up a powerful counter-cathexis to repress his sexuality. As a result, it was impossible for him to reconcile and fuse in one girl his sensual and affectional feelings. When this dynamic became conscious, intense anger emerged toward the mother for rejecting his oedipal bid, for engendering inhibition of sensuality, but also for making him so fearful of losing her love.

Dependence Reactive to Overwhelming Anxiety

When the normal adult is in a situation of overwhelming anxiety, the need for support, for communication increases. A physician of our acquaintance spent his final weeks in a hospital, dying of lung cancer. He knew his condition was hopeless. His wife and his son stayed with him day and night, listening to him offering him moral (i. e., psychological emotional) support. Later, the wife told us, "Doctors have no time for this immense need the patient has for communication, when a human being is all he wants next to him." Both the patient and his wife recognized their helplessness in warding off the inevitable. According to the mourner, the patient's deepest need was for contact and communication. It is probable that the need for communication, or just to have another (specific) human being nearby, is one of the ego's measures to master the anxiety created by the approach of death. In large part, it derives from the need to be protected by an anaclitic object, and its prototype comes from earliest life experiences: the mother-child relationship. The least it represents is the dread of facing death alone. Few men are psychologically equipped to face death alone.

Dependence Reactive to Trauma

A sixteen-year-old girl told her doctor with dismay:

"My grandmother had labyrinthitis. We thought she had a stroke. She blacked out and couldn't see. She was calling for *her* mother! She is sixty-four! She really was sick!"

Regression under anesthesia for surgery is well known. Classical is the case of a business executive who had undergone a cholecystectomy, and who, on coming out of the anesthetic, called for his mother. Environmental stresses, too, may increase one's need and search for protection under the wing of a parental surrogate. For example, soldiers fighting a common enemy very quickly become attached to "the company" or to "the crew."

REACTIONS TO DEPENDENCE

When gratification of dependent needs is ego-syntonic, acceptable to the superego, it produces pleasure. The individual capable of accepting his (not unreasonable) need for objects can be called mature (in Saul's sense), in relation to dependence. But healthy too, is the positively adaptive reaction against dependence seen continually in development, as in the thrust to self-reliance which dependent feelings often induce. On the other hand, many reactions against dependence are negatively adaptive; they solve the problem, but at too costly a price to psychic well-being. We wish to illustrate here reactions *against* dependence. It is at times difficult to make the clinical distinction between reactions *against dependent needs* and reactions *to frustration of dependent needs*. In the first, the wish to reject the need or the state of "feeling needy" is preeminent; in the second, it is the reaction to not having one's needs gratified. Often frustration of the need may lead to rejection of the state of "feeling needy;" both then may be operative in many cases.

Positively Adaptive Reactions: Thrust to Self-Reliance

Signs of autonomy appear early. Very young children often reject a lending-hand (reject dependence) in response to a push to mastery that comes, at least in part, from imitation of and identification with the love object. Thus, a three-year-old boy rejects his mother's offer to tie his shoelaces for him. With a distinct "no," he pretends he is tying his shoelaces and walks about the room showing off the untied shoelaces he has tied in fantasy. Later, he ostentatiously ignores his mother when she sits him on her lap and ties them. A little girl age 34 months, rejects the extended helping hand as she challenges her own anxiety created by the wish to jump from a small table. The anxiety was surmounted by her great effort to master this threatening situation; and she rejected the available hand that would have provided security. It is doubtful whether the child knows at this age, that security from within is a greater preserver of well-being than security from without! While we believe it correct to note these as reactions to dependence, they also represent an impulse to autonomy, to mastery, and we suggest that the rejection of help may come from interference with gratification of the attempt at mastery.

In analysis, Howard M. revealed identification with the analyst which was, in large part, motivated by his shame at being dependent on him. It was evident that this identification, which was syntonic with past identification, served a progressive trend, that of further individuation from the (transference) love-object.

Also, as Howard M. illustrates, loss of self-esteem of any sort allows for two major ways for reparation of that loss: (1) to get love from the object and (2) to effect ego activity that brings one closer to one's idealized self-concepts.

As an example of the latter, Howard M. soon devised a work project which he felt would bring him satisfaction. He was successful and indeed gratified. His behavior was thus self-reliant, and, of itself, raised self-esteem.

The first avenue of reparation from such loss of self-esteem may be regressive, a regression which may be benign or malignant. If benign, as in actively extracting libidinal supplies from objects, it may suggest a variant of "emotional refueling" (Pine and Furer, 1963). Probably most of us need some of this type of "getting" now and then. However, the regression may be such that the individual becomes psychologically dependent to an excessive degree. Thus, an alcoholic, intoxicated as a result of a blow to his self-esteem, needs his wife to undress him and put him to bed, as did his mother years ago, or as she did very seldom. Such regression is reparatory for the alcoholic, but not positively adaptive.

The following case illustrates not a reaction against dependence, but rather a reaction to dependence. It shows how securing an object-tie, essentially by allowing relative gratification of dependence on a stable and predictable object, led to the emergence of a phallic-genital cathexis of that anaclitic object.

Johnny was an eight-year-old boy in treatment twice a week by a fellow in Child Psychiatry who was supervised by one of the authors. In a special therapeutic classroom he was extremely difficult to handle, with severe temper outbursts. When efforts were made to control him physically he spat, kicked, and struggled vigorously. He was, however, not out of contact during outbursts and only minimally destructive. He was rejected by the school as uncontrollable and was taken into treatment provisionally by a therapist who believed that the boy was testing the sincerity of any adult he met to determine the depths of the adult's interest in him. The boy's father had long since disappeared, and his mother had died when he was three. In each of subsequent foster placements, he established a pattern of rejecting those who tried to help him. When he entered treatment, he had been living for over a year with a very religious woman who took him in as she had other foster children, as another creature who needed saving from this evil world. She was able to tolerate his testing probably because of her readiness to bear another burden. He calmed down at home but did very poorly in school.

The therapist who saw him was a young woman with three children of her own who was particularly at ease with preschool and latency-age children. She was warm and could set limits in a positive way. For months, he was reserved. The psychiatrist gradually helped to settle things for him: the social worker was to bring him on time and the therapy sessions were to be kept with regularity; a school arrangement was eventually worked out. In the beginning he gave marked evidence of feminine-identification: when he played house he arranged the furniture, ironed clothes, took the children to the doctor. Eventually the inevitable with this type of child occurred: Johnny asked his therapist to take him home with her. (Note he had been in many foster homes, this was possible in his perception of reality.)

After a year of treatment, Johnny began to suggest in play sessions that he was the father and the therapist the mother. It was striking to see, now, the emergence of an adult male identification in this masculine, sturdily-built boy who had previously exhibited such persistent feminine and dependent activity-attitudes. It was following the appearance of a trusting relationship in which he felt supported and accepted that the male identification with all its phallic-oedipal trimmings emerged in treatment. The trusting relationship could have emerged this quickly and to this degree only if a nucleus of basic trust had evolved much earlier in his life, as it probably had in relation to his mother prior to her death when he was three years old. The sequence and the character of attachment during Johnny's treatment indicated that the genital-sensual cathexis and, with it, the oedipal wishes followed the affectional cathexis of the woman therapist. This, in turn, followed or was closely associated with the fact that he had learned to trust the therapist, who had insured greater stability of his home and school situation and was interested in him.

We have discussed extensively the relation of sensuality to the affectional current of the libido in Chapter 1. In a word, when the child begins to experience phallic-genital impulses, he will expect them to be gratified by the same person who has dominantly gratified his other needs. Sensuality follows the path of the affectional feelings for the primary love-object, in man a path carved by dependence. This path is also used by pregenital sensual needs which are experienced in relation to the object upon whom the child is dependent. They have been so attached since the experience that needs are painful and that much of their gratification is effected by the object.

Negatively Adaptive Reactions

Defense against Dependent Needs. As we noted earlier, the question of whether this defense is a reaction to need or to frustration of need is not always clear. Negative reactions to dependent needs are evidenced by the observable defensive action they induce. A latency youngster may say, "who cares," when he gets D on a report card instead of a love-securing, self-esteem-raising A (love-securing from within as well as from without). He could attempt to assuage the loss in self-esteem by getting love from loved objects; but, not anticipating this, he denies the wish for praise and love from parents as well as the loss of self-esteem. One high school boy rationalized that it was more masculine to get C's than A's.

Here is another example of defense against dependent needs. A teacher in her mid-forties has three adolescents. Two years ago, her husband committed suicide. She is lonely, and on and off feels his absence sharply. She feels drained because, in spite of her regular teaching job and part-time work as an artist, her sister asks her to help with preparations for the Christmas meal. She is angry with her 18-year-old son who doesn't contribute enough money to the household. She says that "money would solve my problem." She attempts to make her emotional situation more tolerable by a defense: although she is by no means financially pressed, she convinces herself that lack of money is the source of her hopelessness, thereby denying the actual cause.

Children who have sustained repeated object loss through separation or rejection may react to offers of help with rejection and denial of dependent needs, libidinal and nonlibidinal. Many children of broken homes, many pre-delinquents, will resist forming a relationship out of fear of again losing a love object and the gratification such an object affords. These youngsters too, out of anger at frustration of needs in the past, use a hostile denial of having any needs. Johnny, our eight-year-old boy, was such a youngster. Helen, a 16-year-old girl, lost her mother at age nine, and her father at age twelve. She was depressed, hostile, and rejecting of peers and adults and rejected help at school where she was doing poorly. In treatment, her most tenacious initial defense was that she needed no one's help: why did she have to come here! Yet, she came alone by bus with regularity, although she was often 10 to 20 minutes late.

Defense against Frustration of Dependent Needs. The following case represents attempts to substitute for the object. Here, as Freud suggested (see Chapter 1) the projected introject (i. e., externalized psychic representation) of the infant's parents is at work; externalizing the idealized introject makes possible the hope of obtaining continued sources of love from without.

A 13-year-old boy's father died in an auto accident three years before the boy entered treatment. The father had been a harsh, immature man who often mistreated his four children. The 13-year-old boy had idealized part of the father by remembering the places the family spent their vacations or the trips they took together. He went into elaborate details of fishing, the lake, the boat, all with highly pleasurable affect. In speaking of his father, he invariably turned to the marvels of "the places father took us." When this was brought to his attention, he grew somber and said, "A lot of times I felt he didn't like me, I don't know why I was so scared of him."

The boy had two representations of his father; the one that came to the surface most readily was the pleasure-yielding father; the second, much defended against, was the hostile, nonloving father. The step that interests us here is that the pleasurable memory of father did not directly include the father, but rather the pleasurable experience father provided for the family. Thus, the place and the activities became cathected, and his yearnings continually turned to wishing he could be at so-and-so fishing, boating; not, wish-father-were-here (that was long unspoken). The object relation was pleasurable so long as it remained vague, and it was rationalized as good because the experiences remembered were good. This case marked the transition of dependence from "on whom" to "on what" (the lake, *the place*; the fishing, *the activity*). This transition in the displacement of the dependence-cathexis took two directions: (1) on an institution; (2) on an activity. To some degree we all do this. Many of our pleasurable object-memories become attached to a place or a thing. "John used to sit in that chair" or, "smoked that pipe." Or, "I love Paris; that is where I met her." But such substitutive cathexes may overextend themselves and become defensive against object relations. Often, of course, we are all realistically dependent for help, not on another person, but on an institution as the hospital, the state.

Affective Reactions to Dependence

Pleasure. Gratification of dependent needs, libidinal and nonlibidinal, leads to pleasure. Pleasure is unimpeded where such gratification is ego-syntonic and thus generally acceptable to the superego. Dependent needs present at all ages and mature self-reliance includes the ability to get one's needs gratified in a reasonable way.

Hurt Narcissism and Shame. We frequently see reactions of shame to being afraid or needing help. Even children are often ashamed if they exhibit transient regressive tendencies. In our middle-class society some parents are embarrassed if their children suck their thumbs, even in infancy, or if they are "shy" or cling to their parents in new situations at the peak age for separation anxiety (from approximately six to 36 mos.). Mrs. B. related that she had been resentful of her 18 month-old child, because friends had remarked that her child's clinging behavior was a sign of her being spoiled. That child, in our presence, suffered episodes of severe separation anxiety which were sharpened in the presence of strangers. To Mrs. B's group of friends, for a toddler to cling means he is "spoiled" which is often handled by shaming.

Libby, a 20-month-old, had returned from a harassing trip for the entire family which included a sojourn with a gravely ill grandmother. In observation, Libby whined and "shadowed" (Mahler, 1965) her mother from the moment she saw us. Mrs. M., tired now from the trip, was embarrassed by Libby's wish to be held. She tried to fend off the child by providing her with toys and sitting down to play with her but refused to pick her up. The child continued to whine, and would not be assuaged verbally. In contrast, Mrs. B. in a similar situation easily understood her child's wish for bodily comfort, allowed the child to climb on her lap with a brief word of recognition and a touch of the hand while she continued to talk to the observers. Cynthia stayed on that lap for five seconds and, emotionally-refueled, slid away laughing, and proceeded with five variations on the theme of "hide and seek." Part of the play included climbing onto mother's lap for intervals of two to five seconds. The game was successful; the anxiety was mastered. One mother allowed her child to be dependent in a most reasonable way; the other was embarrassed by and resentful of her child's need to be held. Another mother could not understand why her three-month-old infant sucked his thumb and said she would not get him a pacifier. If such negative reactions to dependence are engendered in segments of our society in a 20 month-old child, surely shame reactions to dependent needs will present in many adults in that same population.

Generally, the feeling of shame is preceded by hurt narcissism. This readily observable type of sequential dynamic pattern supports Piers and Singer's (1953) formulations referent to the shame-guilt cycle. Recognizing his dependent needs, Howard M. required all the courage he could muster to acknowledge his dependence on the analyst. This acknowledgement was difficult, because it led to a narcissistic devaluation which in turn produced shame.

Howard M.'s analysis revealed clearly two component reactions to feeling dependent in children, adolescents, and adults: (1) the narcissistic wound and feeling small that leads to shame, and (2) the frustration of dependent needs that leads to anger and may in turn lead to guilt. Both reactions, as Piers observed, tend to reinforce each other and may become circular.

Hostility. Hostility is often produced in relation to dependence. The most primitive *reaction to frustration of any need is anger*, as seen in the hungry infant who goes from crying to a rage reaction. We ought perhaps to reserve the word "anger" for a later developmental period inasmuch as we do not ascribe sufficiently differentiated psychic content commensurate with anger in the neonate. We are nevertheless all familiar with the negative quality of the rage-like reaction of the hungry infant.

The older child often responds to withholding of love with feelings of rejection and, if the withholding is stringent enough, with loss of self-esteem leading to resentment, anger, and even rage. Our eight-year-old Johnny who suffered from early and repeated object losses because of frequent changes of foster-home placements, by the time he reached us exhibited rage in reaction to intense feelings of frustration of dependent needs, as well as a defense against involvement. Once secure in a therapeutic relationship he could say: "You make short hours here."

The adolescent or the young adult who is denied love or sexual gratification from his chosen object, often follows a similar pattern: an adolescent whose date rejected his bid for a goodnight kiss, muttered under his breath, "Whore!" His reaction was more than just a reactive hostility to frustration of needs. Here, aggression also served hurt narcissism.

Dependence on another human being for the gratification of needs may *lead to insecurity from which hostility may follow*. Fear of rejection is a frequent experience of childhood. To retain parental love, a child will control disapproved behavior. However, when that behavior is carried out, fear of loss of love frequently leads to insecurity and to resentment toward the object and toward the self.

Often, children who have lost an object of great importance at a period of heightened need will adopt the philosophy of noninvolvement with a new object. Being dependent, loving someone is too hazardous, potentially too painful. They grow anxious when the relationship becomes friendly and may react with hostility. One adolescent, who had lost her mother and father within a two-year period, began to deride, and stopped taking music lessons from, a man toward whom she was beginning to have warm feelings. Her manifest attitude was: "Who needs it!"

As in Richard B.'s case, the valued relationship may be precariously retained, and the need craving gratification may be denied, repressed, or otherwise defended against. Richard B. manifested this by largely denying and inhibiting sensuality in order to retain mother's love. When this dynamic became conscious, intense anger emerged toward the mother: for rejecting his oedipal bid, for engendering inhibition of sensuality, but also for making him so insecure, so fearful of losing her love.

Dependence may lead to a feeling of *lack of freedom* associated with hurt narcissism and hostility. The child who wishes he were already grown, the student who impatiently wants his degree, any man employed by another, is bound by rules and regulations prescribed by the authority upon whom he is dependent, insofar as the authority gives the nod, the degree desired. Frequently, this lack of freedom leads to resentment.

Man is dependent on his government to insure optimal protection of his freedom; he must, in turn, constrain his own actions for the benefit of society. When children resent limitations on their wishes, one can often see the struggle between their impulse and efforts to refrain from gratifying it in order to comply with the parents' wish. The sacrifice leads, however, to anger from which fear of retaliation may follow: "You never let me have anything," said a resentful five-year-old as he walked away from his mother who had just set limits on a third piece of candy. This reaction, of course, was overdetermined, and more serious issues than candy were at stake. The dynamics, however, are the same. The need for love and protection is one of the major forces that civilizes the drives.

Depression. Since the work of Abraham (1916, 1924) and Freud (1917), it is generally accepted that in the dynamics of depression regression occurs to the developmental phase wherein psychologic dependence is maximal—approximately six to 18 months of age, when object loss is experienced most acutely, as suggested by the findings of Mahler (1961, 1966), Spitz (1946b), Bowlby (1960), Jacobson (1964) and others.

Depression is often encountered in response to frustration of dependent needs. The dynamics here may arise from an anaclitic loss (Spitz, 1946b) which leads to feeling unloved, depleted, and unsupported, to reactions variously described as grief, hopelessness and helplessness (Schmale, 1964) and depression-withdrawal (Engel, 1962). (A review of the literature on the relevance of dependence and the loss of the object to depression, is outside the scope of this book.)

SUMMARY

Dependence on the object for gratification of needs is a significant determinant of behavior. The child (and the adult) requires the power of the parent (or authority) to assure him security, provide support under stress, to help him learn to adapt to new situations. To assure "protection, care, and indulgence," the child modifies his behavior, and in this context, his helplessness and dependence is the earliest significant civilizing force.

Man accepts his dependence at times gracefully, at times not. Where daily transient regression occurs in the service of the ego (Kris), libidinal nutriment, serves to revitalize the organism. Many individuals, however, do not mature satisfactorily enough and exhibit too great dependence on objects (for a given developmental stage), or insufficient or defective valuations of objects. Both types lead to maladaptive character formations and represent some of our most difficult psychiatric problems, such as alcoholism, drug addiction, various other forms of pathologic dependent characters, as well as some antisocial character formations and the dramatic childhood psychoses, autistic and symbiotic.

Indeed, where dependence on objects is denied, as in its most extreme and archaic form, autism—where the object is negatively hallucinated away even before denial as a defense can take place—it leads to severe disturbance. Nothing is so hopeless to therapeutic endeavor as the patient who cannot be reached by an object; nothing makes upbringing efforts of parents so fruitless as the child who denies the need for libidinal supplies or protection.

In both normality and pathology, reaction to anxiety by seeking protection from the external environment is an adaptive sequence conditioned from early life. Illness, and other stresses often lead to transient reactions of dependence, with the seeking of protection from the external environment.

The experience of normative dependence in our children is often not accepted by them. And many times, this has salutary effects, as in the child who masters a situation of anxiety by actively repeating it while rejecting help that is offered. By this he rejects the pattern: anxiety → dependence on the auxiliary ego.

Intolerance of normative dependence by parent or child, however, may also have notable ill-effects. Many parents reject dependence in even very young children. This, as well as intolerance of dependence within oneself, may lead to defensive psychic activity such as denial of needs for human relations. Substitutions for need or for objects often are successful and useful; but just as often they miscarry and lead to undue frustration, resentment, and hostility.

Negative affective reactions to dependence are common. We often see hurt narcissism and shame, as well as reactions of hostility. Insecurity and restrictions in development and behavior are a common outcome of such reactions. Intensification of dependence resulting from loss of a love-object contributes significantly to depression. This phenomenon arises from the anaclitic component that exists in all significant object relations.

Dependence then is a significant contributor to the dynamics of psychic life. It is an important determinant of behavior, of affects and moods, of object relations, of the economy of libido and of psychic structure formation.

REFERENCES

Abraham, K. (1924), A Short Study of the Development of the Libido. *Selected Papers of Karl Abraham.* New York: Basic Books, 1953, pp. 418-501.

———— (1925), Character Formation on the Genital Level of Libido Development. *Selected Papers of Karl Abraham.* New York: Basic Books, 1953, pp. 407-417.

Alpert, A. (1959), Reversibility of Pathological Fixations Associated with Maternal Deprivation in Infancy. *The Psychoanalytic Study of the Child,* 14: 169-185. New York: International Universities Press.

Balint, M. (1953), *Primary Love and Psychoanalytic Technique.* New York: Liveright.

Benedek, T. (1949), The Psychosomatic Implications of the Primary Unit: Mother-Child. *Amer. J. Orthopsychiat.,* 19:642-654.

———— (1956), Toward the Biology of the Depressive Constellation. *J. Amer. Psychoanal. Assn.,* 4:389-427.

———— and Rubenstein, B. B. (1942), The Sexual Cycle in Women. Psychosomatic Medicine Monogr. III; 1, 2. Washington, D.C.: National Research Council.

Beres, D. (1956), Ego Deviation and the Concept of Schizophrenia. *The Psychoanalytic Study of the Child,* 11:164-235. New York: International Universities Press.

Bibring, E. (1953), The Mechanism of Depression. In: *Affective Disorders,* ed. P. Greenacre. New York: International Universities Press, pp. 13-48.

Bowlby, J. A. (1958), The Nature of the Child's Tie to His Mother. *Internat. J. Psycho-Anal.,* 39:350-373.

———— (1960a), Separation Anxiety. *Internat. J. Psycho-Anal.,* 41:89-113.

———— (1960b), Grief and Mourning in Infancy and Early Childhood. *The Psychoanalytic Study of the Child,* 15:9-52. New York: International Universities Press.

Brenner, C. (1959), The Masochistic Character: Genesis and Treatment. *J. Amer. Psychoanal. Assn.,* 7:197-226.

Brody, M. W. and Mahoney, V. P. (1964), Introjection, Identification and Incorporation. *Internat. J. Psycho-Anal.,* 45:57-63.

Dubos, R. (1967), Biological Remembrance of Things Past. Presented at the 14th Annual Freud Memorial Lecture of the Philadelphia Association for Psychoanalysis.

Engel, G. L. (1962), Anxiety and Depression-Withdrawal: The Primary Affects of Unpleasure. *Internat. J. Psycho-Anal.,* 43:89-97.

_____ and Reichsman, F. (1956), Spontaneous and Experimentally Induced Depression in an Infant with a Gastric Fistula. *J. Amer. Psychoanal. Assn.,* 4:428-452.

Erikson, E. H. (1950), *Childhood and Society.* New York: W. W. Norton, 2nd ed., 1963.

_____ (1959), *Identity and the Life Cycle.* [Psychological Issues, Monogr. 1], New York: International Universities Press, pp. 1-171.

Fairbairn, W. R. D. (1954), *An Object-Relations Theory of the Personality.* New York: Basic Books.

Fenichel, O. (1945), *The Psychoanalytic Theory of Neurosis.* New York: W. W. Norton.

Freud, A. (1936), *The Ego and the Mechanisms of Defense.* New York: International Universities Press, 1946.

_____ (1947), The Psychoanalytic Study of Infantile Feeding Disturbances. *The Psychoanalytic Study of the Child,* 2:119-132. New York: International Universities Press.

_____ (1952), The Mutual Influences in the Development of Ego and Id. *The Psychoanalytic Study of the Child,* 7:42-50. New York: International Universities Press.

_____ (1954), Psychoanalysis and Education. *The Psychoanalytic Study of the Child,* 9:9-15. New York: International Universities Press.

_____ (1960), Discussion of Dr. John Bowlby's Paper. *The Psychoanalytic Study of the Child,* 15:53-62. New York: International Universities Press.

_____ (1962), Assessment of Childhood Disturbances. *The Psychoanalytic Study of the Child,* 17:149-158. New York: International Universities Press.

_____ (1963), The Concept of Developmental Lines. *The Psychoanalytic Study of the Child,* 18:245-265. New York: International Universities Press.

Freud, S. (1900), The Interpretation of Dreams. *Standard Edition,* 4 & 5. London: Hogarth Press, 1953.

_____ (1905), Three Essays on the Theory of Sexuality. *Standard Edition,* 7:123-243. London: Hogarth Press, 1953.

_____ (1909), Family Romances. *Standard Edition,* 9:236-241. London: Hogarth Press, 1959.

_____ (1912), On the Universal Tendency to Debasement in the Sphere of Love (Contributions to the Psychology of Love, 2). *Standard Edition,* 11:178-190. London: Hogarth Press, 1957.

_____ (1913a), Totem and Taboo. *Standard Edition,* 13:VII-XVI, 1-161. London: Hogarth Press, 1955.

_____ (1913b), The Claims of Psychoanalysis to Scientific Interest. *Standard Edition,* 13:165-190. London: Hogarth Press, 1955.

_____ (1914), On Narcissism: An Introduction. *Standard Edition,* 14:69-102. London: Hogarth Press, 1957.

_____ (1915), Instincts and Their Vicissitudes. *Standard Edition,* 14:111-140. London: Hogarth Press, 1957.

_____ (1917), Mourning and Melancholia. *Standard Edition,* 14:239-258. London: Hogarth Press, 1957.

_____ (1920), Beyond the Pleasure Principle. *Standard Edition,* 18:1-64. London: Hogarth Press, 1955.

_____(1921), Group Psychology and the Analysis of the Ego. *Standard Edition*, 18:67-143. London: Hogarth Press, 1955.

_____(1923), The Ego and the Id. *Standard Edition*, 19:3-66. London: Hogarth Press, 1961.

_____(1924a), The Economic Problems of Masochism. *Standard Edition*, 19:157-170. London: Hogarth Press, 1961.

_____(1924b), The Dissolution of the Oedipus Complex. *Standard Edition*, 19:173-179. London: Hogarth Press, 1961.

_____(1926), Inhibitions, Symptoms and Anxiety. *Standard Edition*, 20:77-174. London: Hogarth Press, 1959.

_____(1927), The Future of an Illusion. *Standard Edition*, 21:3-56. London: Hogarth Press, 1961.

_____(1930), Civilization and Its Discontents. *Standard Edition*, 21:59-145. London: Hogarth Press, 1961.

_____(1933), New Introductory Lectures on Psycho-Analysis. *Standard Edition*, 22:3-182. London: Hogarth Press, 1964.

_____(1937a), Analysis Terminable and Interminable. *Standard Edition*, 23:211-253. London: Hogarth Press, 1964.

_____(1937b), Constructions in Analysis. *Standard Edition*, 23:256-269. London: Hogarth Press, 1964.

_____(1939), Moses and Monotheism. *Standard Edition*, 23:3-137. London: Hogarth Press, 1964.

_____(1940), An Outline of Psychoanalysis. *Standard Edition*, 23:141-207. London: Hogarth Press, 1964.

Fries, M. E. (1946), The Child's Ego Development and the Training of Adults in his Environment. *The Psychoanalytic Study of the Child*, 2:85-112. New York: International Universities Press.

Gray, P. H. (1958), Theory and Evidence of Imprinting in Human Infants. *J. Psychol.*, 48:155-166.

Guntrip, H. (1961), *Personality Structure and Human Interaction.* New York: International Universities Press.

Hammerman, S. (1965), Conceptions of Superego Development. *J. Amer. Psychoanal. Assn.*, 13:320-355.

_____(1966), Lectures. Philadelphia Psychoanalytic Institute.

Harlow, H. F. (1960), Primary Affectional Patterns in Primates. *Amer. J. Orthopsychiat.*, 30:676-684.

_____ & Harlow, M. K. (1962), Social Deprivation in Monkeys. *Scientific American*, 207:136-146.

_____(1966), Learning to Love. *American Scientist*, 54:244-272.

_____ & Zimmerman, R. R. (1959), Affectional Responses in the Infant Monkey. *Science*, 130:421-432.

Hartmann, H. (1939), *Ego Psychology and the Problem of Adaptation.* New York: International Universities Press, 1958.

_____(1950), Comments on the Psychoanalytic Theory of the Ego. *The Psychoanalytic Study of the Child*, 5:74-96. New York: International Universities Press.

_____(1952), The Mutual Influences in the Development of Ego and Id. *The Psychoanalytic Study of the Child*, 7:9-30. New York: International Universities Press.

_____Kris, E. & Loewenstein, R. M., (1946), Comments on the Formation of

Psychic Structure. *The Psychoanalytic Study of the Child*, 2:11-38. New York: International Universities Press.

————— ————— —————(1949), Notes on the Theory of Aggression. *The Psychoanalytic Study of the Child*, 3/4:9-36. New York: International Universities Press.

————— & Lowenstein, R. M., (1962), Notes on the Superego. *The Psychoanalytic Study of the Child*, 17:42-81. New York: International Universities Press.

Hendrick, I. (1942), Instinct and the Ego During Infancy. *Psychoanal. Quart.*, 11:33-58.

Hess, E. H. (1959), Imprinting. *Science*, 130:133-141.

Hoffer, W. (1949), Mouth, Hand and Ego-Integration. *The Psychoanalytic Study of the Child*, 3/4:49-56. New York: International Universities Press.

Jacobson, E. (1954), The Self and the Object World. *The Psychoanalytic Study of the Child*, 9:75-127. New York: International Universities Press.

—————(1964), *The Self and The Object World*. New York: International Universities Press.

Jones, E. (1957), *The Life and Work of Sigmund Freud. V. 3*. New York: Basic Books, 1963.

Levy, D. M. (1954), The Relation of Animal Psychology to Psychiatry. In: *Medicine and Science*, Ed. I. Galdston. New York: International Universities Press, pp. 44-75.

Lichtenstein, H. (1961), Identity and Sexuality. *J. Amer. Psychoanal. Assn.*, 9:179-260.

Liddell, H. S. (1958), A Biological Basis for Psychopathology. In: Hoch, P. H. & Zubin, J., *Problems of Addiction and Habituation*. New York: Grune & Stratton, pp. 94-109.

Lorenz, K. (1935), Companionship in Bird Life. In: *Instinctive Behavior*, Ed. C. H. Schiller. New York: International Universities Press, 1957.

————— (1937), The Nature of Instinct. In: *Instinctive Behavior*, Ed. C. H. Schiller. New York: International Universities Press, 1957.

—————(1953), Comparative Behaviorology. In: *Discussions on Child Development*, eds. J. M. Tanner & B. Inhelder, 1:108-117. New York: International Universities Press.

Mahler, M. S. (1950), Play as a Learning Process. In: *The Exceptional Child in Infancy and Early Childhood. Proceedings of the Conference of the Child Research Center*, Woods School, pp. 28-32.

—————(1952), On Child Psychosis and Schizophrenia: Autistic and Symbiotic Infantile Psychoses. *The Psychoanalytic Study of the Child*, 7:286-305. New York: International Universities Press.

————— (1961), On Sadness and Grief in Infancy and Childhood: Loss and Restoration of the Symbiotic Love Object. *The Psychoanalytic Study of the Child*, 16:332-351. New York: International Universities Press.

————— (1963), Thoughts about Development and Individuation. *The Psychoanalytic Study of the Child*, 18:307-324. New York: International Universities Press.

————— (1965), On the Significance of the Normal Separation-Individuation Phase. In: *Drives, Affects, Behavior*, Vol. 2, ed. M. Schur. New York: International Universities Press, pp. 161-169.

_____ (1966), Notes on the Development of Basic Moods. The Depressive Affect. In: *Psychoanalysis—A General Psychology*, ed. Loewenstein, R. M., et al. New York: International Universities Press, pp. 152-168.

_____ (1967), On Human Symbiosis and the Vicissitudes of Individuation. *J. Amer. Psychoanal. Assn.*, 15:740-763.

_____ (1968a), Annual Conference, Curriculum II, Psychoanalysis of Children, Philadelphia Psychoanalytic Institute.

_____ (1968b), On Human Symbiosis and the Vicissitudes of Individuation. New York: International Universities Press.

_____ & Furer, M. (1963), Certain Aspects of the Separation-Individuation Phase. *Psychoanal. Quart.*, 32:1-14.

_____ _____ & Settlage, C. F. (1959), Severe Emotional Disturbances in Childhood: Psychosis. In: *The American Handbook of Psychiatry*, 1:816-839. New York: Basic Books.

_____ & Gosliner, B. J. (1955), On Symbiotic Child Psychosis: Genetic, Dynamic and Restitutive Aspects. *The Psychoanalytic Study of the Child*, 10:195-212. New York: International Universities Press.

Novey, S. (1958), The Meaning of the Concept of Mental Representation of Objects. *Psychoanal. Quart.*, 27:57-79.

Parens, H. (1970a), A Contribution of Separation-Individuation to the Development of Psychic Structure. In: *Separation-Individuation: Essays in Honor of Margaret S. Mahler*. Eds. J. McDevitt and C. F. Settlage. New York: International Universities Press.

_____ (1970b), Inner Sustainment: Metapsychological Considerations. *Psychoanal. Quart.*, 39:223-239.

Parmelee, A. H. Jr. (1964), A. Critical Evaluation of the Moro Reflex. *Pediatrics*, 33:773-788.

Pearson, G. H. J. (1952), A Survey of Learning Difficulties in Children. *The Psychoanalytic Study of the Child*, 7:322-386. New York: International Universities Press.

Peller, L. (1965), Comments on Libidinal Organization and Child Development. *J. Amer. Psychoanal. Assn.*, 13:732-747.

Piaget, J. (1954), *Les Relations Entre l'Affectivité et l'Intelligence dans le Development Mental de l'Enfant*. Paris: Centre de Documentation Universitaire.

_____ (1962), The Relation of Affectivity to Intelligence in the Mental Development of the Child. *Bulletin Menninger Clinic*, 26:129-137.

Piers, G. & Singer, M. (1953), *Shame and Guilt*. Springfield, Illinois: Thomas.

Pine, F. & Furer, M. (1963), Studies of the Separation-Individuation Phase: A Methodical Overview. *The Psychoanalytic Study of the Child*, 18:325-342. New York: International Universities Press.

Reider, N. (1953), A Type of Transference to Institutions. *Bulletin Menninger Clinic*, 17:58-63.

Ribble, M. A. (1943), *Rights of Infants*. New York: Columbia University Press.

Rosenblatt, J. S., Turkewitz, G. & Schneirla, T. C. (1962), Development of Suckling and Related Behavior in Neonate Kittens. In: *The Roots of Behavior*, ed. E. L. Bliss, New York: Hoebner.

Rosenfeld, S. K. and Sprince, M. P. (1963), An Attempt to Formulate the Meaning of the Concept "Borderline." *The Psychoanalytic Study of the Child*, 18:603-635. New York: International Universities Press.

Sandler, J. (1960), On the Concept of Superego. *The Psychoanalytic Study of the Child*, 15:128-162. New York: International Universities Press.

———Holder, A., & Meers, D. (1963), The Ego Ideal and the Ideal Self. *The Psychoanalytic Study of the Child*, 18:139-158. New York: International Universities Press.

——— & Rosenblatt, B. (1962), The Concept of the Representational World. *The Psychoanalytic Study of the Child*, 17:128-145. New York: International Universities Press.

Saul, L. J. (1947), *Emotional Maturity*. Philadelphia: Lippincott, 1960.

———(1951), *Bases of Human Behavior*. Philadelphia: Lippincott.

———(1967), *Fidelity and Infidelity*. Philadelphia: Lippincott.

——— (1970), "Inner Sustainment": The Concept. *Psychoanal. Quart.*, 39:215-222.

——— & Lyons, J. W. (1952), Acute Neurotic Reactions. In: *The Impact of Freudian Psychiatry*, ed. F. Alexander and H. Ross. Chicago: The University of Chicago Press, 1961.

——— & Pulver, S. E. (1965), The Concept of Emotional Maturity. *Comprehensive Psychiat.*, 6:6-20.

Schmale, A. H., Jr. (1964), A Genetic View of Affects: With Special Reference to the Genesis of Helplessness and Hopelessness. *The Psychoanalytic Study of the Child*, 19:287-310. New York: International Universities Press.

Schneirla, T. C. & Rosenblatt, J. S. (1961), Behavioral Organization and Genesis of the Social Bond in Insects and Mammals. *Amer. J. Ortho.*, 31:223-253.

Schubert, F. (1895), *Songs with Pianoforte Accompaniment*. V. 2. Schirmer's Library of Musical Classics. New York: Schirmer, p. 238.

Schur, M. (1953), The Ego in Anxiety. In: *Drives, Affects, Behavior*, 1, ed., R. Loewenstein. New York: International Universities Press, pp. 67-103.

——— (1960), Discussion of Dr. John Bowlby's Paper. *The Psychoanalytic Study of the Child*, 15:63-84. New York: International Universities Press.

——— (1966), *The Id and the Regulatory Principles of Mental Functioning*. New York: International Universities Press.

Scott, J. P. (1962), Critical Periods in Behavioral Development. *Science*, 138:949-958.

——— (1963), *The Process of Primary Socialization in Canine and Human Infants*. Monographs of the Society For Research in Child Development, 28, No. 1.

Spitz, R. A. (1945a), Hospitalism. An Inquiry into the Genesis of Psychiatric Conditions in Early Childhood. *The Psychoanalytic Study of the Child*, 1:53-74. New York: International Universities Press.

———(1945b), Diacritic and Coenesthetic Organizations. *Psychoanal. Rev.*, 32 (2):146-162.

———(1946a), The Smiling Response: *A Contribution to the Ontogenesis of Social Relations*. Genetic Psychology Monographs, 34:57-125.

———(1946b), Anaclitic Depression: An Inquiry into the Genesis of Psychiatric Conditions in Early Childhood. *The Psychoanalytic Study of the Child*, 2:313-342. New York: International Universities Press.

_____ (1950), Anxiety in Infancy: A Study of Its Manifestations in the First Year of Life. *Internat. J. Psycho-Anal.*, 31:138-143.

_____ (1955), A Note on the Extrapolation of Ethological Findings. *Internat. J. Psycho-Anal.*, 36:162-165.

_____ (1957), *No and Yes*. On the Genesis of Human Communication. New York: International Universities Press.

_____ (1960), Discussion of Dr. Bowlby's Paper. *The Psychoanalytic Study of the Child*, 15:85-94. New York: International Universities Press.

_____ (1965a), The Evolution of Dialogue. In: *Drives, Affects, Behavior*, 2, ed. M. Schur. New York: International Universities Press, pp. 170-190.

_____ (in collaboration with Cobliner, W. G.) (1965b), *The First Year of Life*. New York: International Universities Press.

Waelder, R. (1930), The Principle of Multiple Function: Observations on Overdetermination. *Psychoanal. Quart.*, 5:45-62, 1936.

_____ (1937), The Problem of the Genesis of Psychical Conflict in Earliest Infancy. *Internat. J. Psycho-Anal.*, 18:406-473.

Webster's New International Dictionary (1965), Third Edition. Springfield, Mass.: G & C Merriam Co.

Weech, A. A., Jr. (1966), The Narcotic Addict and "The Street." *Arch. Gen. Psychiat.*, 14:299-306.

Winnicott, D. W. (1953), Transitional Objects and Transitional Phenomena: A Study of the First Not-Me Possession. *Internat. J. Psycho-Anal.*, 34:89-97.

_____ (1965), *The Maturational Processes and the Facilitating Environment*. New York: International Universities Press.

Zetzel, E. R. (1955), Recent British Approaches to Problems of Early Mental Development. *J. Amer. Psychoanal. Assn.*, 3:534-543.

_____ (1965), Depression and the Incapacity to Bear It. In: *Drives, Affects, Behavior*, 2, ed. M. Schur. New York: International Universities Press, pp. 243-274.

INDEX

Abraham, K., 62n, 63, 128, 136, 242
Adaptation
    and affects, 146
    and mastery, 152-153, 232
    and religious beliefs, 28-29
    autonomous and anaclitic, 151, 153
    dependence and, 219, 231-244
    inner sustainment and, 129-133
    models for, 177
    see also Altriciality, Dependence, Ego
Adolescence, 140, 191-198, 201, 214
Adulthood
    early, 199-202
    late, 206-210
    middle, 202-206
Affect
    and adaptation, 146
    and psychic representation, 124
    differentiation of, 166
    see also sub specific affects
Affectional needs, *see* Needs
Aggressive drive, 64, 153n, 161, 176; *see also* Hostility
Alcoholism, dependence in, 5-6, 220-222, 243
Alpert, A., 138
Altriciality, 73, 73n, 86, 98, 100, 100n, 115
    adaptation to, 119, 121, 244
    and dependence, 109, 112, 119-120, 121, 223
    and the period of "insufficient somatopsychic differentiation," 118-119
    in human, 77-78, 111-113, 199

Ambrose, J. A., 96
Anaclitic depression, 146, 148, 167, 170, 242
Anaclitic life condition, 38-39, 120, 122, 136, 200, 203
Anal phase, 62-63, 161-175
Anxiety
    and dependence, 7, 16-35, 243
    and reactive dependence, 223, 227, 230
    see also Separation anxiety, Stranger reactions
Attachment
    in human infant, 75-87, 98, 112-113
    in primates, 98-111
    in precocial neonate, 87, 90-92
    instinctive attachment response, 74, 87, 89
    ". . .the affectionate pre-Oedipus. . ." (Freud), 66, 235
    see also Clinging, Imprinting, Libido, Libidinal object, Object cathexis
Autism, infantile, 6, 220, 243
Autistic phase, 63, 70-83, 86, 161-163
Autoerotic gratification, 162, 165, 169, 176, 188, 195, 201
Autonomy, 151, 187, 197, 199, 232-233; *see also* Primary autonomous ego function
Auxiliary ego, 31, 168, 174, 176, 199, 244
    in late adulthood, 209-210

Balint, M., 8, 78, 116, 138, 162, 163

For Product Safety Concerns and Information please contact our EU
representative GPSR@taylorandfrancis.com
Taylor & Francis Verlag GmbH, Kaufingerstraße 24, 80331 München, Germany